Philip

C000011100

Paper Dolls

a play with music
adapted from the documentary film by
Tomer Heymann

Methuen Drama

Bloomsbury Methuen Drama

An imprint of Bloomsbury Publishing Plc

50 Bedford Square
London
WC1B 3DP
UK

175 Fifth Avenue
New York
NY 10010
USA

www.bloomsbury.com

First published 2013

A catalogue record for this book is available from the British Library

ISBN
PB: 978-1-4725-1127-0
ePub: 978-1-4725-0747-1
ePDF 978-1-4725-0560-6

Typeset by Country Setting, Kingsdown, Kent CT14 8ES
Printed and bound in Great Britain

About the Tricycle

The Tricycle Theatre first opened in 1980 and has established itself as one of London's most significant theatres. West End and Broadway transfers include the Olivier Award-winning productions *The 39 Steps* and *Stones in His Pockets*. Open seven days a week, the Tricycle not only comprises a unique 235-seat theatre, but also an independent 300-seat cinema, vibrant bar and café, plus three rehearsal spaces used for creative learning and community work. Today, with Indhu Rubasingham as Artistic Director, the Tricycle continues its reputation for presenting the highest quality British and international work, that reflects the diversity of its local community.

Indhu Rubasingham's inaugural show *Red Velvet* won two Critics' Circle Awards and an Evening Standard Award. *The Arabian Nights*, which The Guardian called, 'a beguiling piece of storytelling for family audiences', continued to reflect the Tricycle's commitment to showing the world through different lenses. Most recently the Tricycle played host to Eclipse Theatre Company 's entertaining revival of Don Evans' *One Monkey Don't Stop No Show*.

Paper Dolls is the final production in Indhu's first season as Artistic Director.

'What an incisive, fervent beginning. Indhu Rubasingham takes over with panache at the Tricycle, bowing to the theatre's politically engaged tradition but giving it a sharp new turn.' *Susannah Clapp, The Observer, 21 Oct 2012*

Message from the Artistic Director

Welcome to the final show of my first season. I'm really thrilled to be directing this play which I first read over a year ago. For me, it epitomises my vision for the Tricycle as an ambitious new play, exploring the collision of different cultures, sexualities, religions and languages. It presents an unheard voice on the stage and offers a theatrical insight into a unique world. It's been a real pleasure to collaborate with Philip Himberg, whose work and vision I have respected since before I came to the Tricycle. I do hope you enjoy it and thank you from everyone here at the Tricycle for your support.

Indhu Rubasingham, Artistic Director

PAPER DOLLS

BY PHILIP HIMBERG

A NEW PLAY WITH MUSIC

Adapted from the documentary film by Tomer Heymann

World Premiere

Presented by the Tricycle Theatre in association with
Stanley Buchthal and Bob & Co, Ltd

Cast

in alphabetical order

Yossi	Tom Berish
Yael	Jane Bertish
Ester / Female Ensemble	Noa Bodner
Chaim	Harry Dickman
Chiqui	Ron Domingo
Nazari / Male Ensemble	Ilan Goodman
Male Ensemble	Shimi Goodman
Sally	Francis Jue
Male Ensemble	Tom Oakley
Zhan	Angelo Paragoso
Jiorgio	Jon Norman Schneider
Adina	Caroline Wildi
Cheska	Benjamin Wong

Creative Team

Director	Indhu Rubasingham
Designer	Richard Kent
Lighting Designer	Oliver Fenwick
Sound Designers	Ben & Max Ringham
Music	Nigel Lilley and Ben & Max Ringham
Choreographer	Alistair David
Video Designer	Dick Straker
Voice/Dialect Coach	Richard Ryder
Fight Director	Rachel Bown Williams of Rc-Annie
Assistant Director	Sam Pritchard

DEVELOPED IN PART BY
THE SUNDANCE INSTITUTE
THEATRE PROGRAM
SUNDANCE
INSTITUTE

Philip Himberg Artistic Director
Christopher Hibma Producing Director

Ron Domingo, Francis Jue and Jon Norman Schneider are appearing
with the permission of UK Equity, incorporating the Variety Artistes' Federation.

With support from Kobler Trust, and NoraLee and Jon Sedmak

Production Manager	Shaz McGee
Company Stage Manager	Alison Rich
Deputy Stage Manager	Mary O'Hanlon
Assistant Stage Manager	Helen Stone
Costume Supervisor	Natasha Ward
Casting Director	Will Burton CDG
	for David Grindrod Associates
Press Representation	Emma Holland PR
Set Construction	Russell Carr MBTproductions.co.uk
Production Assistant	Russel Martin
Costume Assistant	Elodie Louis
Wigs Supervisor	Carole Hanock
Model Assistant	Rachel Stone
Head of Lighting	Charlie Hayday
Head of Sound	Mike Thacker
Lighting Programmer	Jack Knowles
Board Operator	Ben Jones
Sound Operator	Tess Dacre
AV Programmer	Dan Bond
Wardrobe Mistress	Tara Stroud
Crew	James Bentley, Scott Carter, Elz,
	Andy Furby, Ben Reeves, Kate Stokes

Media Partner

The Tricycle would like to thank Stick and the Royal Court Theatre,
Dave Cork for his patience and expertise, Donmar Warehouse,
National Youth Theatre, Ruth Parry, Hum, Rachel Writer,
Eve Collins, Phillipa Downes.

A special thanks to Janice Paran for providing dramaturgical support
during US workshops and development of *Paper Dolls*.

PHILIP HIMBERG | WRITER

Since 1997, Philip has served as the Artistic Director of the Sundance Institute Theatre Program.

PAPER DOLLS was commissioned by the Sundance Institute and received developmental workshops at Sundance and the Public Theatre in New York. Previously, Mr Himberg co-wrote and directed the world premiere of CARRY IT ON, with and for singer/actor Maureen McGovern (Arena Stage, the Huntington Theatre, Geva Theatre, and Two Rivers). He directed the world premiere of Terrence McNally's SOME MEN at the Philadelphia Theatre Company and William Finn's SONGS OF INNOCENCE AND EXPERIENCE at Lincoln Center, as well as the West Coast premiere of Tony Kushner's ONLY WE WHO GUARD THE MYSTERY SHALL BE UNHAPPY starring Sally Field. His L.A. production of William Finn's ELEGIES was its West Coast premiere. For Sundance Summer Theatre, he directed revivals of FIDDLER ON THE ROOF, FUNNY GIRL, DEAR WORLD. His essay, *Family Albums*, appears in the Dutton Anthology, GIRLS WHO LIKE BOYS WHO LIKE BOYS.

Philip is currently President of the Board of Trustees of Theatre Communications Group, the umbrella service organisation for over 700 not for profit American theatre companies and the home of ITI/US.

THE CAST

TOM BERISH

Theatre includes: THE TAMING OF THE SHREW (RSC); OF MICE AND MEN (Watermill); FAMILY BUSINESS (Watford Palace Theatre/ Oxford Playhouse); ROMEO AND JULIET (Royal Lyceum); ARE WE NEARLY THERE YET? (Wilton's Music Hall); AFTER THE END (Battersea Arts Centre); LINES (Rosemary Branch).

Television includes: DOCTORS, THE LAST HEROES OF D-DAY, THE VILLAGE (BBC).

Film includes: FINDING TIME by Miranda Howard-Williams.

JANE BERTISH

Theatre includes: HOUSE OF BERNADA ALBA (Almeida); A ROUND HEELED WOMAN (Riverside Studios/ West End); THE SYNDICATE (Chichester/ Tour); NICHOLAS NICKLEBY (Chichester/ West End/ Toronto); A FAMILY AFFAIR (Arcola); TALES FROM VIENNA WOODS (National); DUCHESS OF MALFI (West Yorkshire Playhouse); THE WHITE DEVIL, THE MILKTRAIN DOESN'T STOP HERE ANYMORE (Lyric, Hammersmith); JUDITH (Traverse/ BAC/ Tour); CONVERSATIONS WITH MY FATHER (Old Vic); PHAEDRA (Aldwich/ Old Vic); NO END OF BLAME, THE LAST SUPPER, SEVEN LEARS, GOLGO (Royal Court); MOTHER COURAGE (Mermaid); ANATOL AND WALPURGISNACHT (Gate); BRIGHT ROOM CALLED DAY (Bush).

Television includes: ASHES TO ASHES, SENSITIVE SKIN, FRENCH AND SAUNDERS, EASTENDERS, SINS, THE PASSION, BROKERS MAN, VANITY FAIR, CASUALTY, THE LENNY HENRY SHOW (BBC); LEWIS, INSPECTOR MORSE, SAM SATURDAY, LIFE AFTER LIFE (ITV); SWORD OF HONOUR (CH4).

Film includes: THREE; DANCE WITH A STRANGER; SMART MONEY; PAPERHOUSE; PARKER; THE REEF; THE ROMAN SPRING OF MRS STONE.

NOA BODNER

Theatre includes: A MIDSUMMER NIGHT'S DREAM (World Tour), FLOYD COLLINS (Southwark Playhouse); JUDENFREI (New End Theatre); THE FOOL (Cock Tavern); THE HOUSE OF MIRRORS & HEARTS (Arcola & Edinburgh Festival); MAY CONTAIN NUTS (Hen and Chickens, Islington); LATIN FEVER (West End/ Tour); A LITTLE NIGHT MUSIC, THE BAKER'S WIFE, THE IMPORTANCE OF BEING EARNEST, FALLEN ANGELS (Royal Academy); HAIR-LIVE IN AHOY (UK/ Holland); TELEMACHUS CLAY, ONCE UPON A MATTRESS, THE HOSTAGE, MY FAIR LADY, HAIR (Library Theatre Israel); LES MISERABLES (Israeli Opera House).

Television includes: ROME (BBC/HBO); THE NUCLEAR RACE, ELTON JOHN GALA CONCERT AT THE ROYAL OPERA HOUSE (BBC).

Film includes: WORLD WAR Z (Paramount Pictures); THE CROSSMAKER; CHATROOM (Pathé/Ruby Films).

HARRY DICKMAN

Theatre includes: THREE SISTERS (Young Vic); TRAVELLING LIGHT (FILM SEQUENCE) (National Theatre), AS YOU LIKE IT (Theatre Clwyd); LAST OF THE SUMMER WINE (UK Tour); STEPTOE & SON (Comedy Theatre & Theatre Royal, York); SCROOGE (Bill Kenwright); SHAMLET (Edinburgh Fringe); FIDDLER ON THE ROOF (UK Tour); DUCK VARIATIONS (Bridewell Theatre); LITTLE SHOP OF HORRORS (Landor Theatre); 42ND STREET (UK Tour); DICK WHITTINGTON (UK Productions); PIRATES OF PENZANCE (UK Productions); TALE OF TWO CITIES (Bill Kenwright); THE FANTASTICKS (Metaphor Productions).

Television includes: ANY HUMAN HEART (Channel 4); DOCTORS (BBC); ALL ABOUT GEORGE (Granada); MR CHARITY (BBC); THE THINGS YOU DO FOR LOVE (Granada).

Film includes: NATIONAL TREASURE 2.

Currently celebrating 52 years in show business.

RON DOMINGO

Theatre in the USA includes: THE ROMANCE OF MAGNO RUBIO (Ma-Yi Theatre, OBIE Award); THE AMERICAN PILOT (Manhattan Theatre Club); THE KING AND I (Harbor Lights Theatre Company); A DREAM PLAY (Cleveland Playhouse); ON HOUSE (WPA Theatre).

Television includes: BLUE BLOODS, PERSON OF INTEREST, AS THE WORLD TURNS, RESCUE ME (CBS); PAN AM, LAW & ORDER (NBC).

Film includes: TENDERNESS; ROBOT STORIES; THE MOTEL; SLOW JAM KING.

ILAN GOODMAN

Theatre includes: RED LIGHT WINTER (Theatre Royal Bath); TARTUFFE (English Touring Theatre); CHICKEN SOUP WITH BARLEY (Royal Court); DANTON'S DEATH (National); MISS NIGHTINGALE (The Lowry/ Kings Head Theatre); SIX DEGREES OF SEPARATION (Old Vic); BRIDGET JONES THE MUSICAL (Original workshop production for Working Title); BREAKING THE SILENCE, ALL QUIET ON THE WESTERN FRONT (Nottingham Playhouse); AUSTENTATIOUS (Landor Theatre); THE GLASS MENAGERIE (New Wolsey Ipswich).

Television includes: YES, PRIME MINISTER (BBC); LOST COSMONAUTS (Discovery Channel).

Film includes: A LONG WAY DOWN; DIANA; THAT WOMAN; THE ECHELON CONSPIRACY.

SHIMI GOODMAN

Theatre includes: A MIDSUMMER NIGHT'S DREAM, RAGTIME (Regent's Park Open Air Theatre); THE WHO'S TOMMY (The English Theatre, Frankfurt); CHICAGO (Cambridge Theatre); SINGIN' IN THE RAIN (Broadway studio); EVITA (Tour); INTO THE WOODS (Gatehouse); PARTY TIME, MOUNTAIN LANGUAGE (Landor); DIRTY DANCING (Aldwych); CHICAGO (Adelphi); BOMBAY DREAMS (Apollo Victoria); ANYONE CAN WHISTLE (Bridewell); SALT & HONEY (Mount Scopus Amphitheatre, Jerusalem); CARMEN (Rosin Centre, Tel Aviv).

Television includes: SKINS (E4).

Film includes: LIFT; A RESOLUTION.

Music recordings include: WHEN YOU HEAR MY VOICE; STANDING OVATION; HEY PRODUCER!; DIRTY DANCING (Original London Cast); ATTIC.

FRANCIS JUE

Theatre in the USA includes: Broadway: PACIFIC OVERTURES, THOROUGHLY MODERN MILLIE, M. BUTTERFLY.

Off-Broadway: YELLOW FACE (Obie and Lucille Lortel Awards), LOVE'S LABOUR'S LOST, HAMLET, AND A LANGUAGE OF THEIR OWN (Public Theatre); CORALINE (MCC Theatre); FALSETTOLAND (National Asian American Theatre); NO FOREIGNERS BEYOND THIS POINT (Ma-Yi Theatre).

Regional: IN THE NEXT ROOM OR THE VIBRATOR PLAY (Actors Theatre of Phoenix, Zoni Award); MISS SAIGON (Muny Theatre, Judy Award); INTO THE WOODS, KISS OF THE SPIDERWOMAN (Drama-Logue Award), CABARET (Bay Area Critics Circle Award), FLOYD COLLINS (TheatreWorks); RED (Wilma Theatre); THE ILLUSION, A MIDSUMMER NIGHT'S DREAM (Arizona Theatre Co.); THE WINTER'S TALE (Yale Rep); THE KING AND I (American Music Theatre of San Jose).

Television includes: THE GOOD WIFE (CBS); LAW & ORDER: SVU, LAW & ORDER (NBC).

Film includes: JOYFUL NOISE.

For Papa.

TOM OAKLEY

Theatre includes: WEST SIDE STORY (RSC - Sage Gateshead); JERSEY BOYS (Prince Edward Theatre); LOVE NEVER DIES (Adelphi Theatre); ONCE UPON A TIME AT THE ADELPHI (Liverpool Playhouse); PETER PAN (Civic, Chelmsford); BEST FRIENDS AND BUTTERFLIES (Shoreditch Festival 2008); HELLO AGAIN (George Wood Theatre); MORE OR LESQUE; ALADDIN (Newbury Corn Exchange).

Other work includes: Lead vocalist at WHATSONSTAGE AWARDS 2009 (Prince of Wales); London Show Choir for OUR LADY J (Royal Festival Hall); Vocalist with The Adelphi Crew at the Liverpool Echo Arena; Writer/ Composer/ Orchestrator/ Producer/ Director/ MD of new musical 'RiZen' along with Daniel Finn (Rogue Studios); Djembe/ Piano/ Lead/ Backing Vocals - The Kilderkins SINGING SONGS & RAISING FUNDS; Piano/Vocals – Third Time Lucky BRAZILIAN SESSIONS, Piano – Doll Mechanics SLEEP WELL IN VIENNA, Composer – '(LOUDLY) IN A QUIET ROOM'; Vocalist – SIR BILLI (Sarm Studios, Sascha Hartmann); Vocalist, HAMLET 2.

Film includes: MISSING CHRISTMAS.

ANGELO PARAGOSO

Theatre includes: MISS SAIGON (UK No. 1 Tour); THE REPORTER (National); PEARLS OF THE EAST (Pinoy Theatre); THE KING AND I (Royal Albert Hall); ALADDIN (Theatre Royal Stratford East); PETER PAN (Manchester Opera House); MISS SAIGON, FAME (Netherlands Production).

Opera includes: DOCTOR ATOMIC (English National Opera).

Radio includes: THE HONOURABLE SCHOOLBOY, THE SECRET PILGRIM, WRITING THE CENTURY: TIGER WINGS (BBC Radio 4).

JON NORMAN SCHNEIDER

Theatre in the USA includes: A MAP OF VIRTUE (13P); QUEENS BOULEVARD (the musical) (Signature); DURANGO (The Public); CHING CHONG CHINAMAN (Pan Asian Rep); A PLAY ON WAR, BLIND MOUTH SINGING (NAATCO); EDITH CAN SHOOT THINGS AND HIT THEM (Actors Theatre of Louisville/ Humana Festival); POOL BOY (Barrington Stage); AMERICAN HWANGAP (Magic); DURANGO (Long Wharf); CITIZEN 13559: THE JOURNAL OF BEN UCHIDA (Kennedy Center).

Television includes: VEEP (HBO); 30 ROCK, LAW & ORDER: CRIMINAL INTENT (NBC); THE ELECTRIC COMPANY (PBS).

Film includes: THE NORMALS; THE REBOUND; ANGEL RODRIGUEZ.

CAROLINE WILDI

Theatre includes: NOISES OFF (Old Vic); MUCH ADO ABOUT NOTHING, ROMEO AND JULIET (RSC); I AM A CAMERA, MAKING DICKIE HAPPY (Rosemary Branch); MANSFIELD PARK (Chichester Festival Theatre); PRIVATE LIVES, THE GHOST TRAIN, BLITHE SPIRIT (Queens Theatre Hornchurch); THE WOMAN WHO COOKED HER

HUSBAND (Chester Gateway); THE DICE HOUSE (Coventry Belgrade); A J RAFFLES (Watford Palace); THE 39 STEPS, HAY FEVER, DEATH TRAP, JOKING APART, TAKING STEPS, CHORUS OF DISAPPROVAL, VOYAGE AROUND MY FATHER, SALAD DAYS (Southwold); THE ADMIRABLE CRICHTON (Haymarket Theatre Royal); TING TANG MINE, FATHERS AND SONS (National).

Television includes: HEREAFTER, IF I HAD YOU (ITV); EASTENDERS (BBC), BROOKSIDE (CH4).

Film includes: DEUX FRERES; HARRY POTTER AND THE HALF-BLOOD PRINCE.

BENJAMIN WONG

Theatre includes: THOROUGHLY MODERN MILLIE (Watermill); THE KING AND I (Theatre at the Mill, Northern Ireland); FIREWORK MAKER'S DAUGHTER (UK No. 1 Tour); INTO THE WOODS, HAGRIDDEN (Embassy Theatre); WIZARD OF OZ (Drama Centre); MOONBIRD (Esplanade); DEATH & DANCING (Play); SHELTER (Action Theatre), HAMLET (Fort Canning Park); TO KILL A MOCKINGBIRD (Victoria Theatre).

Music includes: THE 12 TENORS (German Tour); THE 12 INTERNATIONAL TENORS (European Tour); J.S. BACH CANTATA 21 (St John Church), BAROQUE FESTIVAL (Victorian Arts Centre).

Awards include: Best Newcomer in DEAD MAN JUMPING (Action Theatre); Best Supporting Actor in DOCTOR, DOCTOR ! (Victoria Theatre); Honorary Mention in The Singer of the Year Award, Australia.

THE CREATIVE TEAM

INDHU RUBASINGHAM | DIRECTOR

Indhu is Artistic Director of the Tricycle. She was recently awarded the Arts & Culture Award at the Asian Women of Achievement Awards for 'astounding achievements in theatre'. Indhu was awarded the Carlton Multi-Cultural Achievement Award for Performing Arts and in 2010 she jointly received the Liberty Human Rights Arts Award for *The Great Game: Afghanistan*. She has previously been Associate Director of The Gate Theatre, Birmingham Rep and The Young Vic.

For the Tricycle Theatre: RED VELVET; WOMEN, POWER AND POLITICS; STONES IN HIS POCKETS; DETAINING JUSTICE; THE GREAT GAME: AFGHANISTAN; FABULATION; STARSTRUCK.

Other selected directing credits include: BELONG, DISCONNECT, FREE OUTGOING, LIFT OFF, CLUBLAND, THE CRUTCH, SUGAR MUMMIES (Royal Court); RUINED, (Almeida); YELLOWMAN, ANNA IN THE TROPICS (Hampstead Theatre); THE WAITING ROOM (National Theatre); THE RAMAYANA (National Theatre/ Birmingham Rep); SECRET RAPTURE, THE MISANTHROPE (Minerva, Chichester); ROMEO AND JULIET (Festival Theatre, Chichester); PURE GOLD (Soho Theatre); NO BOYS CRICKET CLUB, PARTY GIRLS (Stratford East); WUTHERING HEIGHTS (Birmingham Rep); HEARTBREAK HOUSE (Watford Palace); SUGAR DOLLIES, SHAKUNTALA (The Gate); A RIVER SUTRA (Three Mill Island Studios); RHINOCEROS (UC Davies, California) and A DOLL'S HOUSE.

RICHARD KENT | DESIGNER

Upcoming work includes: THIS IS MY FAMILY (Sheffield Crucible).

Recent work includes: THE DANCE OF DEATH (Trafalgar Studios); JOSEPHINE HART POETRY WEEK (ARTS); MACBETH (Sheffield Crucible); 13 (NYMT, Apollo); CLOCKWORK (Hightide Festival); TITANIC – SCENES FROM THE BRITISH WRECK COMMISSIONERS INQUIRY: 1912 (MAC Theatre, Belfast); RICHARD II (Donmar Warehouse); MIXED MARRIAGE (Finborough); STRONGER AND PARIAH (Arcola).

Richard has worked as Associate to Christopher Oram since 2008, working on numerous shows at the Donmar Warehouse including: SPELLING BEE, KING LEAR (also BAM, New York), PASSION, RED (also Broadway and Mark Taper Forum, LA), A STREETCAR NAMED DESIRE as well as IVANOV, TWLEFTH NIGHT, MADAME DE SADE, (Donmar West End) and HAMLET (DWE, Elsinore Denmark and Broadway).

Other work as Associate includes: DON GIOVANNI (Metropolitan Opera); MADAME BUTTERFLY (Houston Grand Opera); BILLY BUDD, NOZZE DI FIGARO (Glyndebourne); COMPANY (Sheffield Crucible); DANTON'S DEATH (National); EVITA (Broadway).

OLIVER FENWICK | LIGHTING DESIGNER

For the Tricycle Theatre: RED VELVET; POISON; THE CARETAKER.

Theatre includes: THE HOLY ROSENBERGS, HAPPY NOW? (National); THE WITNESS, DISCONNECT (Royal Court Theatre); MY CITY, RUINED (Almeida);THE WINTERS TALE, THE TAMING OF THE SHREW, JULIUS CAESAR, THE DRUNKS,THE GRAIN STORE (RSC); BERENICE, HUIS CLOS (Donmar); AFTER MISS JULIE (Young Vic); SAVED, A MIDSUMMER NIGHT'S DREAM (Lyric, Hammersmith); THE KINGDOM OF EARTH, FABRICATION (The Print Room); THE BEGGARS OPERA (Regent's Park Theatre); THE MADNESS OF GEORGE III, GHOSTS, KEAN, THE SOLID GOLD CADILLAC, SECRET RAPTURE (West End); THE KITCHEN SINK, THE CONTINGENCY PLAN, IF THERE IS I HAVEN'T FOUND IT YET (Bush); A NUMBER (Menier Chocolate Factory); PRIVATE LIVES, THE GIANT, GLASS EELS, COMFORT ME WITH APPLES (Hampstead); HAMLET, THE CARETAKER, COMEDY OF ERRORS (Crucible Theatre, Sheffield).

BEN & MAX RINGHAM
SOUND DESIGN AND MUSIC PRODUCTION

Theatre and Performance work includes: A TASTE OF HONEY, RACING DEMON, HAMLET, AN ENEMY OF THE PEOPLE (Sheffield Crucible); SCENES FROM AN EXECUTION, SHE STOOPS TO CONQUER, HENRY IV pts I & II (National); THE MOTOR SHOW (LIFT); BEN HUR (Watermill); WHAT THE BUTLER SAW (Vaudeville); THE DUCHESS OF MALFI, ALL ABOUT MY MOTHER (Old Vic); DEMOCRACY (Sheffield Crucible/ Old Vic); A CHRISTMAS CAROL (Arts Theatre); THE LADYKILLERS (Gielgud Theatre); PAINKILLER (Lyric Belfast); THE ELECTRIC HOTEL (Fuel Theatre); GLORIOUS (Rajni Shah Productions); SALOME (Headlong); POLAR BEARS, PHAEDRA (Donmar Warehouse); THE LITTLE DOG LAUGHED (Garrick); THREE DAYS OF RAIN (Apollo

West End); PIAF (Donmar/ Vaudeville/ Buenos Aires); CONTAINS VIOLENCE (Lyric Hammersmith); THE CARETAKER (Sheffield Crucible/ Tricycle/ Tour); THE ARCHITECTS, AMATO SALTONE, WHAT IF...? TROPICANA, DANCE BEAR DANCE, THE BALLAD OF BOBBY FRANCOIS (Shunt); THE PIGEON (BAC).

Ben and Max were nominated for a Best Sound Design Olivier for PIAF, THE LADYKILLERS and as part of the creative team accepted a 'Best Overall Achievement in an Affiliate Theatre' Olivier award for THE PRIDE.

NIGEL LILLEY | MUSICAL DIRECTOR

Nigel Lilley studied at King's College London and the Royal Academy of Music, where he was the recipient of the DipRam award. In 2011 he was elected an associate of RAM.

Upcoming Work includes: CHARLIE AND THE CHOCOLATE FACTORY (Drury Lane).

Theatre includes: MY FAIR LADY, COMPANY (Sheffield Crucible); RAGTIME (Regent's Park); THE UMBRELLAS OF CHERBOURG (Leicester Curve/ West End); SWEET CHARITY (Menier/ Theatre Royal, Haymarket); SPRING AWAKENING (Lyric Hammersmith/ Novello); LA CAGE AUX FOLLES (Menier Chocolate Factory/ Playhouse); PIAF (Donmar); THE BACCHAE (National Theatre of Scotland); SINATRA (London Palladium); LES MISÉRABLES (Denmark and Bournemouth Symphony Orchestra); Philip Quast at the Donmar (Divas season).

Television includes: PANTO! (ITV); MUSICALITY (CH4).

Nigel has enjoyed regular collaborations with Victoria Wood on projects including THAT DAY WE SANG (Manchester International Festival), THE GIDDY KIPPER (Sky), ERIC AND ERNIE and VICTORIA WOOD'S CHRISTMAS SPECIAL (BBC), TALENT (Menier Chocolate Factory) and ACORN ANTIQUES (Tour). He is co-author of the audition handbook *Thank you, that's all we need for today,* published by Peter Edition.

ALISTAIR DAVID | CHOREOGRAPHER

Theatre includes: MY FAIR LADY, THE WAY OF THE WORLD, MY DAD'S A BIRDMAN, BULL (Sheffield Theatres); POSH (West End); THE SOUND OF MUSIC (Regent's Park Open Air Theatre); THE GOLDEN AGE OF BROADWAY (Southbank Centre); ONCE UPON A TIME IN WIGAN (Paines Plough/ Hull Truck); A BOWL OF CHERRIES (Charing Cross Theatre); THOROUGHLY MODERN MILLIE, RADIO TIMES (Watermill/ Tour); THE SLEEPING BEAUTY (Sheffield Lyceum); ANYTHING GOES (Arts Educational); NICKED (HighTide Festival); BELLS ARE RINGING (Union Theatre, 2011 'Best Choreographer' Off West End Award); FASCINATING AIDA (Theatre Royal Haymarket); BAT BOY, FOOTLOOSE, ROMEO & JULIET: THE ROCK OPERA); CINDERELLA (Oxford Playhouse); ALADDIN, SLEEPING BEAUTY (Theatre Royal Bath); SNOW WHITE (Theatre Royal Hull); A CHORUS LINE, WEST SIDE STORY, SEVEN BRIDES FOR SEVEN BROTHERS (Cambridge).

Television includes: THE LATE LIST (CH4); BIG TIME RUSH WEEK (Nickelodeon); MY SUPER SWEET 16, BUSTAMOVE, THE LAUREUS WORLD SPORTS AWARDS (MTV).

DICK STRAKER | VIDEO DESIGNER

For the Tricycle Theatre: SEIZE THE DAY.

Theatre includes: A MARVELLOUS YEAR FOR PLUMS (Chichester); GOING DARK (Fuel Theatre); THE LESSENING OF DIFFERENCE (South East Dance); ORPHEUS AND EURYDICE (National Youth Theatre Old Vic Tunnels); TRISTAN AND ISOLDE (Grange Park Opera); FAT GIRL GETS A HAIRCUT (The Roundhouse); TIGER COUNTRY (Hampstead); THE KING AND I (Leicester Curve); DESIRE UNDER THE ELMS (New Vic Staffordshire); TALES OF BALLYCUMBER (Abbey Theatre Dublin); IT'S A WONDERFUL LIFE (Wolsey Theatre Ipswich); THE MOUNTAINTOP (Trafalgar Studios); JUST ADD WATER?, FAULTLINE (Shobana Jeyasingh Dance Company); RUSHES (Royal Ballet); THE RING CYCLE (ROH); SUGAR MUMMIES, HITCHCOCK BLONDE (Royal Court); JULIUS CAESAR (Barbican/ Tour); RICHARD II (Old Vic); THE WOMAN IN WHITE (Palace Theatre London / Marquis Theatre NY); HIS DARK MATERIALS, HENRY V, THE COAST OF UTOPIA, SOUTH PACIFIC (National); Jumpers (National / Piccadilly Theatre / Brooks Atkinson NY); THE DUCHESS OF MALFI, THE POWERBOOK (National/ Tour).

RICHARD RYDER | VOICE AND DIALECT COACH

For the Tricycle: RED VELVET.

Theatre includes: THE WINSLOW BOY (Old Vic Theatre); ONE MONKEY DON'T STOP NO SHOW (Eclipse Theatre); THIS HOUSE, PORT, COCKTAIL STICKS AND HYMN (National Theatre); THE TURN OF THE SCREW (Almeida Theatre); UNCLE VANYA (Vaudeville Theatre); THE 39 STEPS (Criterion Theatre and Tour); I CD ONLY WHISPER (Arcola Theatre); MY FAIR LADY, A TASTE OF HONEY (Crucible, Sheffield); THE KINGDOM (Soho Theatre); BEAUTIFUL BURNOUT (Frantic Assembly); WAR HORSE (New London Theatre); WAH! WAH! GIRLS (Sadlers Wells); THE NORMAN CONQUESTS (Liverpool Everyman); TWIST OF GOLD (Polka Theatre); WONDERFUL TOWN (Manchester Royal Exchange).

Television includes: BOUND (Tiger Aspect); HOLBY CITY (BBC).

Film includes: GAMBIT.

Richard has worked in the voice department of the RSC and is currently a member of the National Theatre voice department.

www.therichervoice.com

SAM PRITCHARD | ASSISTANT DIRECTOR

Sam trained as a director on the MFA at Birkbeck, University of London and the NT Studio Directors Course. He is the winner of the JMK Award for Young Directors 2012.

Directing credits includes: FIREFACE (Young Vic); GALKA MOTALKA (Royal Exchange Studio); MONEY MATTERS (Nabokov / Soho Downstairs); THE PARROT HOUSE (Liverpool Everyman/ Everyword Festival).

He was the New Writing Associate at the Royal Exchange 2010 and 2012, where he ran the theatre's new writing programme and the Bruntwood Prize for Playwriting 2011.

WILL BURTON CDG for DAVID GRINDROD ASSOCIATES CASTING DIRECTOR

Current West End/other includes: MATILDA; ONCE; A CHORUS LINE; VIVA FOREVER!; SHREK; THE COMMITMENTS; MAMMA MIA! (Worldwide); JESUS CHRIST SUPERSTAR (Arena Tour).

Touring and regional includes: MY FAIR LADY (Sheffield Crucible); SECRET GARDEN (Edinburgh/ Toronto); CHICAGO, GHOST, HAIRSPRAY, HIGH SOCIETY (UK Tours).

Film includes: UK Dancer Casting : NINE – directed by Rob Marshall; Ensemble Casting : MAMMA MIA! – directed by Phyllida Lloyd; THE PHANTOM OF THE OPERA – directed by Joel Schumacher.

Television includes: SUPERSTAR (ITV); OVER THE RAINBOW (Talkbackthames); I'D DO ANYTHING, ANY DREAM WILL DO, HOW DO YOU SOLVE A PROBLEM LIKE MARIA (BBC, 2007 EMMY AWARD); KOMBAT OPERA PRESENTS…(BBC2, 2008 Golden Rose Montreux Award); HOLLYOAKS (CH4) WEST END STAR (TV3 Sweden).

David Grindrod Associates are members of The Casting Directors Guild of Great Britain.

Paper Dolls
**produced by the Tricycle Theatre
in association with Stanley Buchthal and Bob & Co, Ltd.
Developed, in part, by the Sundance Institute Theatre Program**

STANLEY BUCHTHAL

Stanley Buchthal is an international entrepreneur in fashion, finance and media. He has a USA based company called Dakota Group Ltd and a Swiss based production company LM Media GmbH.

Stanley produced or executively produced the following films: LOVE, MARILYN (Director: Liz Garbus); MARINA ABRAMOVIC: THE ARTIST IS PRESENT (Directors: Matthew Akers & Jeff Dupre); BOBBY FISCHER AGAINST THE WORLD (Director: Liz Garbus); JEAN-MICHEL BASQUIAT: THE RADIANT CHILD (Director: Tamara Davis); HERB & DOROTHY (Director: Megumi Sasaki); LOU REED'S BERLIN (Director: Julian Schnabel); BLACK WHITE + GRAY: A PORTRAIT OF SAM WAGSTAFF AND ROBERT MAPPLETHORPE (Director: James Crump); THE AMERICAN RULING CLASS (Director: John Kirby); UP AT THE VILLA (Director: Philip Haas); SPANKING THE MONKEY (Director: David O.Russell); HAIRSPRAY (Director: John Waters); PAUL BOWLES: THE CAGE DOOR IS ALWAYS OPEN (Director: Daniel Young) and WATCHERS OF THE SKY (currently in post-production, Director: Edet Belzberg).

BOB & CO

Bob & Co is a media advisory firm that provides guidance, fundraising and investment in film, television and theatre projects, and whose Executive Directors and principle shareholders are Bob Benton and Simon Flamank.

Bob & Co counsel companies on a range of issues such as brand management, corporate strategy and business planning, non-executive directorships, fund-raising and industry introductions.

The media investment and development aspect of the business focuses on finding promising content and getting it to production. With the desire and ability to invest in the right people, Bob & Co puts direct investment in emergent media companies, and individual investments in the development of film, theatre and television projects.

Bob and Simon each have over 20 years' experience in both media advisory roles and the market itself; operating investment and entertainment companies at an executive level both in the UK and overseas. Simon and Bob met through their work together at Handmade Films in 2010, where their efforts led to the necessary restructuring and subsequent sale of the company.

THE SUNDANCE INSTITUTE THEATRE PROGRAM

The Theatre Program has been a core component of Sundance Institute since Robert Redford founded the Institute in 1984. The Theatre Program is renowned for supporting the development of writers, composers and other artists of the stage, and shepherding their plays. Under the guidance of Artistic Director Philip Himberg and Producing Director Christopher Hibma, the Sundance Institute Theatre Program is recognised as one of the leading play development programs in the United States. Titles such as SPRING AWAKENING, I AM MY OWN WIFE, GREY GARDENS, THE LIGHT IN THE PIAZZA, THE LARAMIE PROJECT, CROWNS, CIRCLE MIRROR TRANSFORMATION and PASSING STRANGE are among the hundreds of plays nurtured at Sundance. The Theatre Program hosts a range of creative labs and workshops annually in the U.S., and around the world, including the Theatre Labs at the Sundance Resort, Mass MoCA, White Oak Plantation, and Ucross, Wyoming. The Theatre Program's International Initiative in East Africa is a decade old, and is the only professional program of its type on the continent, offering cross-cultural exchange, residencies and exposure to artists in six African countries. A new Middle East/North Africa Initiative is currently in its initial planning stage.

SUPPORT US

The Tricycle Theatre has always been a pioneer and a risk-taker. As we herald a new chapter, your support will help us to continue this bold tradition during uncertain economic times. Membership contributions and donations play a vital role in supporting our ambitious artistic programme and Creative Learning projects with young people in the local community.

'We believe deeply in all the work it does both artistically and educationally'
Primrose and David Bell, Tricycle members since 1996

With your support

- We can continue to push boundaries artistically across stage and screen, building on the success of productions such as the critically acclaimed and award winning *Red Velvet* and *Great Game: Afghanistan*.

- Our Creative Learning and award-winning targeted projects will engage with even greater numbers of children and young people, helping to inspire a new generation through theatre and creative writing.

Join us today

'I like the atmosphere, like supporting the values of the Tricycle, and enjoy coming with friends.'
Steven Baruch, Tricycle member since 2004

Our members receive the very best benefits across stage and screen, with invitations to member events, priority booking, and opportunities to observe and participate in Creative Learning workshops.

Membership starts from just £125 per year. To join and for further details, please visit www.tricycle.co.uk, phone the Development Department on 020 7625 0132 or email **development@tricycle.co.uk**.

Thank you in advance for your support

£125+ *Trailblazer*

Be the first to hear about our theatre and cinema programme, with priority booking and regular newsletters

Join us through invitations to members' events

Experience stage and screen with ticket offers, free ticket exchange, complimentary cinema tickets and theatre programmes

Be part of the action with an invitation to our annual Creative Learning day

Thank you with a membership card and acknowledgement on the website

£500+ *Innovator*

All the above benefits, plus:

Experience stage and screen with reserved theatre seating and use of the Cinema Box

Get even closer to the action with invitations to targeted project performances

Thank you in the theatre programme and personal ticket booking

£1250+ *Pioneer*

All of the above benefits, plus:

Be the first with season press releases and access to sold out shows

Experience stage and screen with signed theatre programmes and additional reserved theatre seating

Exclusive access with invitations to behind-the-scenes and Artistic Director events

A special thank you with acknowledgement on the supporters' board

£3000+ *Director's Circle*

Make a lasting difference to the future of the Tricycle by joining our Director's Circle. Director's Circle members enjoy all of the above benefits plus enhanced privileges, exclusive to this higher level. From supper with the Artistic Director, complimentary tickets and backstage tours, Director's Circle members will be offered the opportunity to get closer to and truly engage with the Tricycle.

Thank you

The work we produce at the Tricycle Theatre would not be possible without the support of our individual donors, trusts and foundations and corporate partners. We are extremely grateful to all those who have continued to support us this year and over the last financial year.

Trusts & Foundations

AB Charitable Trust
Ardwick Charitable Trust
Aspect Charitable Trust
Austin & Hope Pilkington Trust
Barcapel Foundation
The Bertha Foundation
Brown-Mellows Trust
Catkin Pussywillow Charitable Trust
95.8 Capital FM's Help a Capital Child
Concertina Charitable Trust
The Coutts Charitable Trust
SNR Denton UK LLP
D'Oyly Carte Charitable Trust
John Ellerman Foundation
The Ernest Cook Trust
Esmée Fairbairn Foundation

Equity Charitable Trust
Foresters' Friendly Society
Garfield Weston Foundation
Garrick Charitable Trust
Robert Gavron Charitable Trust
The Goldsmiths' Company
Guildford Academics Association
The Ernest Hecht Charitable Foundation
Government of Ireland
Irish Youth Foundation
Kobler Trust
Little Charity
John Lyon's Charity
The MacArthur Foundation
Mackintosh Foundation
The Mercers' Company

Posgate Charitable Trust
David & Elaine Potter Foundation
Sigrid Rausing Trust
Joseph Rowntree Charitable Trust
The Henry Smith Charity
Sir Siegmund Warburg Voluntary Settlement
The Sobell Foundation
The Stanley Foundation
The Topinambour Trust
Unity Theatre Trust
Vanderbilt Family Foundation
Vandervell Foundation
Royal Victoria Hall Foundation
Harold Hyam Wingate Foundation
The Worshipful Company of International Bankers

Individuals

Major Donors
Charles Diamond
Jonathan & Lucy Silver
Annette Stone & Anthony Van Laast
Al & Joan Weil

Director's Circle
Sir Trevor & Lady Susan Chinn

Pioneers
Liz Astaire
John Reiss
Jonathan Tyler

Innovators
Henry Chu & James Baer
Posgate Charitable Trust
Rajeev Samaranayake

Front Wheels
AKA Promotions Ltd
David & Jenny Altschuler

Primrose & David Bell
Jennie Bland
Helen & Keith Bolderson
Katie Bradford
Fiona Calnan
Kevin Clancy
Kay Ellen Consolver & John Storkerson
Michael Farthing & Alison McLean
Michael Frayn
Frankie de Freitas
Gillian Frumkin
Grete Goldhill
Nick Gray
Lady Hatch
Alan & Mary Hobart
Sir Christopher Hogg
Sarah Ingham
Miki Jablkowska
Anya & Grant Jones
Bob & Kate Kaplan
Judy Lever
Jake Levy

Zander Levy
Jeremy Lewison & Caroline Schuck
Andrée Molyneux
Diana & Allan Morgenthau
Valerie Pike
Alan Rickman
Peter Roth
Michael & Gail Sandler
Professor Philippe Sands
Marjorie & Albert Scardino
Carol Sellars
Professor Aubrey Sheiham
Barbara Sieratzki
Jon Snow
Jenny & Lawrence Stolzenberg
Peter Wilson
Peter Wolff
Joseph & Sarah Zarfaty

Benefactors
S Ashcroft
Helen Fraser

Alan & Judith Harding
Tony & Melanie Henderson
Harold & Valerie Joels
David Lubin & Tamara Joffe
John & Margaret Mann
Jackie Rothenberg
Marjorie & Anthony Simonds-
  Gooding
Rosalyn & Nicholas Springer
Nick Viner & Victoria Boyarsky
Nicolas Warren & Catherine
  Graham-Harrison

Supporters
Colin Adams & Mary Farrell
David & Francine Altaras
Steven & Sharon Baruch
Debbie Behrens
Mr & Mrs Berman
Mr & Mrs Binstock
Jack Black
Martin Blackburn
Rosemary Bradley
Alan Brodie Representation Ltd
Kate Brooke
Kenneth E Brown
Jules Burns
Mary Callaghan
James Carroll & Dycella
  Cummings-Palmer
Jim Carter

Jessica Clark
James Coakes
Mrs L Colchester
Cooper-Hohn Famiy
Mr & Mrs R Dantzic
Arnold Desser
Lily & Anthony Filer
Sally Fleming
Sue Fletcher
Deirdre Flood
S Gilbert
Sybil Goldfoot
Rosita & Brian Green
Martyn Gregory
Peter Guter
Charles & Jenny Henry
Barbara Hosking
Barry Jackson
Christine Jackson
Gareth James
Stephen Jellis
Margaret Johnson
Christopher Knowles & Mary Anne
  Bonney
David Lanch
Isabelle Laurent
Peter Levy
R Lloyd & K Bouchane
Virginia Makins
Simon & Pauline Malpas
Alexi & Michael Marmot

Liz Marsh
Geoff Mayne
Lyn Meadows
Ruth & Paul Miller
Jim Minton
Tangy C Morgan
Michael & Jenny Nathan
Richard Norton-Taylor
Dr & Mrs Papadakis
Damien Patel
Nancy Platt
I G & B Rappaport
Michael & Sandi Richman
Geoffrey Robertson QC
Michael Robinson
Dr Joan Schachter
Christine Scholes
Lois Sieff OBE
Guy Slater
Brian Smith
Pauline Swindells
Patricia Tatspaugh
Peter Tausig
Mrs Tynan
Judith Farbey & Prabhat Vaze
Richard Walton
Steve & Sandar Warshal
Lavinia Webb
Janet Weitz
JGW
Ros & David Wright

The Tricycle would also like to thank the Friends and all anonymous donors

Cinema Box Members
Parvez & Lena Ahmed
Steven & Sharon Baruch
Jim Broadbent
David Cohen
Veronica Cohen
Richard Curtis
Gerry & Kim Davis
Fiona Finlay
Roda Fisher & Michael Hannaway
Maggie Gee
Jack Gold
Bird & Alan Hovell
Gillian Howard
Isabel J Hudson

Gemma Jackson
J Anna Jansz
Ann & Gerard Kieran
Christopher Kitching
Jenifer Landor
Monique Law
John & Rose Lebor
Marilyn & Victor Lownes
Liz Mace
M P Moran & Sons Ltd
Isabel Morgan
Terry Munyard
Gina Newson
Vince Power
Michael & Sandi Richman

Catherine Roe
John & Melanie Roseveare
Michael & Margaret Rustin
Philip Saville
Glenis Scadding
Isabelle & Ivor Seddon
Barrie Tankel
Scott Tearall
Emma Thompson
Eliana Tomkins
Maggie Turp
Sandar Warshal and Family
Christine & Tom Whiteside
Michael Winner
Jeffrey Woolf OBE

We also want to thank our corporate partners, whose generosity allows us to pursue our innovative artistic programme and to work with children and young people in the local community. Opportunities for corporate partnership include production sponsorship, funding a social inclusion workshop, or supporting another element of the Tricycle's work on stage or screen, with benefits for both the company and staff. Please contact the Development Department on 020 7625 0132 for further details.

Corporate Partners

Bloomberg

HSBC

Alliance Publishing Press
Blick Rothenberg Chartered Accountants
British American Drama Academy
Casareccia
The Clancy Group
Daniel and Harris Solicitors
J. Leon & Company Ltd
JPC Law
London Walks Ltd
Mulberry House School
The North London Tavern
Samuel French Ltd

We are enormously grateful to the members of our Development Committee, who volunteer their expertise and experience by advising on and supporting the Tricycle's fundraising activities.

Kay Ellen Consolver (Co-Chair); Judy Lever (Co-Chair); Lesley Adams; Nadhim Ahmed; Baz Bamigboye; Andrew Daniel; Sally Doganis; Kobna Holdbrook-Smith; Grant Jones; Mairead Keohane; Jonathan Levy; Jeremy Lewison; Rupert Lord; Andree Molyneux; Allan Morgenthau; Caroline Phillips; Michael Sandler; Christine Scholes; Caroline Schuck; Geraldine Sharpe-Newton; Sue Summers.

CREATIVE LEARNING

We are committed to working with and inspiring young people from the local community to express themselves creatively.

Our Creative Learning programme reaches a large number of young people, offering workshops, engagement with professional artists, and opportunities to perform on stage. Whether these are young people with a passion for performance, developing self-esteem, or in search of identity and a sense of community - the theatre is theirs, and they are the future audiences and artists.

Our popular workshops cater for young people up to the age of 25, with our successful Tricycle Young Company featuring some of the theatre stars of the future.

The Tricycle's award-winning targeted projects include **Minding the Gap**, the leading national project working with young newly arrived refugees and asylum seekers who are not yet in school. Meanwhile, at **Press Road** we work with young people who are gang affected on the Press Road Estate. Both embrace theatre, art and creative writing to establish a sense of community and celebrate diverse cultures.

Such commitment to the local community and unheard voices requires serious investment, and membership contributions play a vital role in ensuring the future of our education and social inclusion projects. If you would like to pledge your support towards a specific project, please call the Development Department on 020 7625 0132.

'The Tricycle Theatre has provided a very valuable service to these vulnerable children and often the first words that children speak in English are in the Tricycle sessions.'
Teacher, Greenway Project, Minding the Gap

'I don't recall having so much fun since I first saw James Corden in One Man Two Guvnors. *It was theatre with a passion.'*
***Daily Mail,* July 2012, Minding the Gap performance**

'Working together with Tricycle Theatre this Autumn, we have helped tackle key issues surrounding anti-social behaviour on the estate and helped improve community cohesion by improving our youth provision.'
Lucy Revill, Community Engagement and Investment Officer, Network Stadium, Press Road

For the Tricycle

Artistic Director	Indhu Rubasingham
Executive Director	Kate Devey
Director of Finance and Operations	Bridget Kalloushi
Technical Director	Shaz McGee
Artistic Associate	Nic Wass
Associate Producer	Zoe Ingenhaag
Marketing Director	Holly Conneely
Senior Marketing Officer	Alice Wright
Marketing Assistant	Ben Carruthers
Development Director	Tom Mullion
Development Officer	Lisa Morlidge
Administrative Manager	Trish McElhill
Acting Creative Learning Director	Anna Myers
Creative Learning Manager	Mary Chilton
Finance Officer	Lise Bell
Finance Officer	Jane Pollendine
Cinema Programmer	John Morgan Tamosunas
Projectionist	Michael Rose
Relief Projectionist	S R Gobin
Archivist (Voluntary)	Anne Greig

Front of House

Front of House Business Manager	Gail Deacon
House Managers	James Foran, Andy Orme, Owen Sampson
Relief House Managers	James Bush, Paul Carstairs, Tara Kane, Michael O'Kelly, Elliot Taylor
Box Office Manager	Tom Nolan
Assistant Box Office Manager	Emma Faulkner
Box Office Supervisors	Michael Byrne, Joanna Beattie

Front of House Team

Tolu Alaka
Maks Andala
Olivia Armstrong Long
Enrico Aurigemma
Brodie Baker
Simona Bitmate
Miles Brown
Jessica Clark
Leah Cox
Keiron Craven-Grew
Jane Crawshaw
Daniel Essongo
Rodolphe Fleury

Jeremy Fowler
Neil Glassman
Mary Guerin
Steve Hines
Caitlin Hoskins
Chris Hughes
Tariq Jordan
Emma Kizintas
Alice Lee
Danielle Nott
Hillary Pierce
Clare Pointing
Francesco Ponzo

David Porter
Jennifer Majka
Joshua Manning
John Sheil
David Stroud
Tara Stroud
Ben Victor
Niamh Webb
Alex Williams
Emily Mae Winters
Siobhan Witter
Jasmine Yoloye

Introduction

Spring 2006. I am sitting in a darkened movie theatre in Los
Angeles to see *Paper Dolls*, a brand-new Israeli documentary
film premiering at the LA Film Festival. It would go on to win
the festival's Audience Award in the weeks ahead. The film is
described as the story of five Filipino men who emigrate from
Manila to Tel Aviv to work as care-givers to elderly Orthodox
and Chasidic men. On their infrequent days off from work,
they form a kind of homespun singing group dressing up as
drag divas.

The film begins, and director Tomer Heymann vividly
conjures his experiences meeting Chiqui, Jiorgio, Cheska,
Zhan and Sally, and their subsequent travails as strangers in a
strange land. I find myself riveted. It is not the novelty of the
cross-dressing elements that fascinated me; after all, I am a
gay man, well versed in drag culture. What moved me was the
fiercely contemporary and provocative story about the search
for home, and the bravery around crossing borders, both
literal and metaphoric.

The film concludes and I sprint down the aisle, to introduce
myself to Mr Heymann and propose – somewhat inarticulately,
I must admit – that what he had so beautifully rendered as
a documentary film might translate into a live theatrical play.
I explain that I am the artistic director of the Sundance
Institute Theatre Program, known for its development of new
stage work. He seems frankly more perplexed than interested
and points me to another gentleman standing at the back of
the auditorium. 'That is the film's producer. Maybe talk to
him.' Stanley Buchthal, who financed the film, is immediately
intrigued and that week we begin negotiations to move forward.

Initially I planned to commission a playwright I knew to
undertake an adaptation. But what became clear over months
and then years was that my own passion for the story of the
Paper Dolls was greater than that of anyone I might entreat
to join me on this journey. A few months later, I travel to

Tel Aviv where in six hours, a dubious Tomer Heymann transforms from 'Who are you?' and 'What do you want?' to a gracious and enthusiastic host, shepherding me across the city on the back of his motorbike to see each location that was part of the film's setting: the Yemenite neighbourhood of Chiqui's flat, the community of B'nei Brak (which could stand in as a movie set for eighteenth-century Jewish Poland) and the gay clubs. I meet his mother. In a day, we are friends. A year later, I bring Mr Heymann to my own developmental theatre to meet and discuss in more detail his personal investment in the story and characters. He urges me 'to make the play my own' and provides valuable background and stories. And on the way home from Tel Aviv, I stop in London, where many of the actual Paper Dolls now live and work. Meeting them raises the stakes for me: how do I honour the lives of real people?

In February 2010, I spend eighteen days in the cold but stunning landscape of north-eastern Wyoming, at the Sundance Playwrights Retreat at Ucross. The luxury of a writing studio, and having all my meals prepared for me, make it possible to focus, to unravel the documentary structure and begin to reimagine how a theatrical and dramatic journey might be articulated. In eighteen days, I have a first (bad) draft.

Now, three years later, twenty-five drafts are behind me, and following two workshops with actors, I am back in London, for the world premiere of *Paper Dolls*. My friend and colleague, Indhu Rubasingham, the new artistic director of the Tricycle, has read my script a year ago, and enthusiastically invited me to premiere the play at her theatre. For over ten months we have collaborated, via Skype, over our mobiles and in person to clarify and heighten the story. In the last six weeks, we've worked intensely with an incredibly gifted cast and collaborators to bring *Paper Dolls* to you, in its world premiere.

My aspiration is to honour the universe of these remarkable men who were the subjects of Tomer's movie and to open their astonishing lives to an audience. To me, the Paper Dolls perfectly represent something critical about the world in which we now all reside. Chiqui, Jiorgio, Cheska, Zhan and Sally are the Magellans, the DeSotos, the Vasca de Gamas, the Sir Walter Drakes of our times, compelled to abandon what is familiar and to seek what human beings so desperately desire: community, adventure, understanding, love, family. And in so doing, they enlighten and enrich the world in countless ways − for all of us.

Philip Himberg

Paper Dolls

dedicated to the memory of
Salvador 'Sally' Camatoy

Acknowledgements

The author wishes to thank:

Caroline Aaron, Mujtaba Ahmed, Deborah Asiimwe,
Fanny Ballantine-Himberg, Joan Barber, Henry Russell
Bergstein, Yuval Boim, Billy Bustamante, Sharon Dynak,
Ignacia Delgado, Oran Eldor, Oskar Eustis, Vadim Feichtner,
Alan Filderman, Julie Freestone, Ben Graney, Adam Greenfield,
Mandy Hackett, Jessica Hagedorn, Barak Heymann, Noa
Heymann, Christopher Hibma, Lady Imelda, Lauren Klein,
Will Lang, Telly Leung, Erik Lieberman, Jana Llynn, Jake
Manabat, Lynn McCullough, Orville Mendoza, Max Posner,
Keri Putnam, David Ross, John Rua, Ariel Shafir, Matthew
Wilkas, Doug Wright, the Public Theater, and the Sundance
Institute.

Support with translation: Ron Domingo, Oran Eldor,
Dr Lily Kahn, Angelo Paragosa, Ralph Pena, Ellen Perecman.

The author received support for *Paper Dolls* during a writer's
residency at the Ucross Foundation, Ucross, Wyoming.

A very special thanks to director Mark Brokaw, and to Janice
Paran (dramaturg extraordinaire), who shepherded two
workshops and many drafts of *Paper Dolls* through development
in the US. Also to Stanley Buchthal for his ongoing advice
and enthusiasm, and to Tomer Heymann who imagined there
was a story here.

And above all: to Neil Datinginoo, Chiqui Diokno, Jiorgio
Diokno, Angela Libas, Efrenito Manalili, Francisco Ortiz Jr,
and Paper Dolls everywhere.

Note on the Music

The Dolls' musical numbers are sung to instrumental tracks, as if they are singing karaoke-style. The exceptions to this are 'Hatikvah', 'Rumania, Rumania' and 'Umagang Kay Ganda', which are sung *a cappella*. The Chasid Chorus may sing *a cappella* or to pre-recorded tracks as desired. 'Turning Japanese' is the *only* lip-synched number.

Song titles are supplied in the text, and the style (recordings) from which they are adapted. The Song List (page 94) provides the authorship and music publisher for each song.

Characters

None is biologically transsexual. They are gay men, cross-dressing – more subtly at some times than others – and living lives as close to that of a woman's identity (physically) as they can, as that's how they feel, and depending on their situation – whether they are at work or play. They dress alternately as women and as men, but their male attire is decidedly feminine – hip-hugging jeans, and blousy tops. Scarves. All of them have long hair, earrings. They are all Filipino, and so of course speak Tagalog, but also decent Hebrew and English. They are all solidly 'working class'. Outsiders.

Sally   Thirty-eight years old. Living in Israel eight years. Mature, serious-minded when at work, sensitive and articulate, eager to learn. Deeply spiritual (Catholic). Very responsible, but can rock out and be as crazy as the next when in drag, and loves performing. Talented drag performer with a unique style and 'star' quality. A deep and open-hearted caretaker. She takes care of Chaim.

Chiqui   Thirty-eight years old, the official 'manager' of the Paper Dolls. Not as gorgeous perhaps as the rest, but can be a pretty damn hot woman when he dresses up. He knows how to maximise for best effect. He takes care of an old Chasid man, but does not live with him. He left home at seventeen, spent ten years in Saudi Arabia. Tons of street smarts. Knows the world. Kind-hearted. Looks after his younger brother, Jiorgio. The most practical of the Dolls. There is a seriousness and sadness deep inside but he can be quite playful. He knows the stakes.

Zhan   Twenty-seven years old, seven years in Israel. He is a bit of a follower, defined in large part by his weight: he's tubby, and sweet, big round face, and giggly. He very much needs the group, depends on them as family. They adore him. He has a heart of gold, but a very naughty side as well. He is quite shy even on stage, but loves being up there more than anything.

Just wants to be included. Takes care and lives with a very old Chasidic man.

Cheska   Thirty-five years old, newly arrived in Israel. Very handsome, taller than the others, very long, silky, thick black hair. Can look elegant in a white suit, or sexy as all get-out in a bustier and fishnets. Choreographer for the group. Big olive eyes. Kind warm heart. Polite. A natural innocence, respected by the group for his talent, and his loyalty. First to help a friend.

Jiorgio   Twenty-five years old, Chiqui's younger brother. The rebel. More selfish than the rest, because he has an older brother watching out for him. Starts off as a care-giver but becomes a haircutter. On stage, the most outrageous, he even shocks the other Dolls with his material. Can be abrasive and crazy, but underneath, very vulnerable, and dependent on his brother, though too proud to say it. Knows his make-up and wigs.

OTHER CHARACTERS

Yossi   Early thirties. An Israeli documentary filmmaker. Just beginning a career and hungry. Gay, masculine, handsome, very casual, sexy. Struggling as an artist in a chaotic society. Ego-driven, but raised with a real heart. Born in Israel, the youngest of five sons. Eager to make his mark. Ambition hides his vulnerability. He guards himself with a kind of machismo, perhaps fearful of what is underneath.

Yael   Mid-sixties. Yossi's mother. No-nonsense woman who has lived in Israel all her life, raised five sons mostly on her own, and like many Israelis of her generation says what she thinks. Not a 'New York' Jew; her father was a German who came to Palestine, where she was born, in the early 1930s. Raised on a kibbutz. She is an Israeli through and through – rooted, strong and warm. And in the end, a Jewish mother.

Chaim   Eighty-three years old and suffering from cancer. Sally's client and lives with Sally. Can no longer speak easily due to throat surgery, but has become excellent at expressing himself with gestures, and sometimes when he is emotional his voice makes a 'raspy' articulation if he needs it. He always keeps a pad and pen nearby so he can communicate. An intellectual who prizes his books and classical music above all else. He is a modern Orthodox man, not a Chasid; spiritual, not religious. Very well read. Up on current events. Alone in Israel since his daughter lives in America. He depends on Sally to make his life work.

Adina   Fifty-four. Chaim's daughter. Divorced. Israeli woman who moved from Israel to New York in 1997, and returns now for a visit, seven years later. Her only son, Ezra, died eight years ago. She says what she thinks. The world has left her a bit bitter, a bit dazed. Assertive Israeli. Guarding a broken heart.

Nazari   A thirty-something Israeli out to make a buck. Knows the system. Good-looking, sexy. Runs one of the most successful gay clubs in Tel Aviv, and aspires to be big in Europe as a DJ/party planner. A go-getter. Selfish. (*Note:* also doubles as a Chasid Chorus, London Deejay, and others.)

The Chasid Chorus

Ensemble of three who play many other roles:

Male 1   Israeli Solider at Airport, Policeman, Pageant Announcer, Young Chasidic Man

Male 2   Immigration Official, DJ, Yaakov, Male Prison Guard.

Female   Ester, Female Prison Administrator, Airport Announcer.

The play is set in Tel Aviv in 2004.

Act One

An open stage with several distinct playing areas and levels.

Suggested design motif of Bauhaus era.

Tel Aviv apartments with shutters that can slide open and closed, revealing scenes or tableaux, and serving as projection surfaces for film images.

Pre-set: projections of Hebrew newspaper headlines fill the stage.

Darkness.

Solo klezmer clarinet intro.

Prologue: a 'choreography' of Hebrew headlines. for example:

לוק לארשי

היינשה, הרגס לארשי תנידמ היתולובג תא סידבועל סיניטסלפ.
תנשב 2001תליחתב הדאפיתניאה

הנידמה תותלד תא לארשי תלשממ החתפ סתוא ףילחהל ידכ
סירז סידבוע 300,000-מ רתויל

During the above graphic, lights reveal:

Chorus of Four Chasids *in silhouette.*

Chasids *sing a legato and haunting version of song/prayer, 'Shir La'ma'alot'.*

Suddenly, loud noise of a jet plane landing on the tarmac.

Then:

Recorded Loudspeaker Voice (*female, in Hebrew first; then English overlays and takes over*) Brukhim haba im linmal te'ufa Ben Gurion . . .Welcome to Ben Gurion International Airport. Please have your passport, visa and other paperwork ready for the immigration officials. Stand behind the red line. Do not step forward, until you are called by an Israeli official.

During above announcement we see:

A nervous young Filipino man – **Cheska**. *His long silky black hair is tucked under a 'Carnaby Street'-type hat.*

He walks from up to downstage, pulling a roller bag behind him. He stops when the voice says: 'Stand behind the red line.'

An Israeli **Soldier** *in full uniform with machine gun stands to one side.*

To the other side, an **Immigration Official** *in an immigration 'booth'.*

Cheska *waits.*

Immigration Official (*gestures to* **Cheska**)   Step forward. Your passport. Visa.

The **Official** *looks at the papers for a bit.*

Cheska *stands nervously. He is trying his best to look 'butch'. He clears his throat.*

He glances over at the hunky Israeli **Soldier**. *The* **Soldier** *stares back, shifts his stance. A weird flirtation. This cat-and-mouse game goes on for a while.*

Immigration Official   Where in the Philippines are you from?

Cheska (*softly*) Las Pinas.

Immigration Official   What? Speak up.

Cheska (*trying to modulate his voice and make it lower*)   Las Pinas.

He looks over at the **Soldier**, *who adjusts his belt.*

Immigration Official   You are here to work as – (*Looking at paperwork.*) 'A care-giver' . . . a private nurse?

Cheska (*distracted, staring at* **Soldier**)   What? Oh! Yes. I have work. The agency found me the position.

Immigration Official   And your position was secured where?

Cheska   In Manila. The name of the agency is here –
(*Pointing.*) On this letter. (*He gets nervous.*) I have a job. They have
placed me. With a Mr . . . Cohen.

Immigration Official   We have many Mr Cohens.

Cheska   Mr *Isaac* Cohen in Tel Aviv.

Immigration Official (*sarcastic*)   Oh, *that* Mr Cohen.

Cheska   I have the address. (*He digs in his pocket and presents
crumpled paper.*) And here is the receipt from the agency. I paid
them a fee.

Immigration Official   You understand your visa is valid
only as long as Mr Isaac Cohen employs you?

Cheska   Yes. And I am very happy to be here. I am going to
work very hard.

Immigration Official   I see. (*Not rushing, looking up and down
at* **Cheska**.) You have someone meeting you?

Cheska   Yes, my friend, Chiqui. He has also a job here. Six
years now.

Cheska *nervously steals glances at the* **Soldier**.

The **Official** *hands back the passport, papers, slowly.*

There is a pause, where **Cheska** *does not know if he's passed
inspection. The* **Official** *glances from* **Soldier** *to* **Cheska**.
Cheska *looks at* **Soldier** *and back at* **Official**.

The **Official** *makes a small smile, nods. Pause, finally:*

Immigration Official (*to* **Cheska**)   Welcome to Israel.

Cheska *grabs his big roller bag. It falls over. His long hair falls free
of his hat. He hastily departs, glancing back at* **Official**.

Sudden loud music.

Lights.

The immigration booth turns into a DJ booth.

And the **Immigration Official** *is now a* **DJ**.

Three weeks later.

A disco / party atmosphere. Smoke, bodies dancing, singing.

Intro to 'Venus' under (Bananarama).

DJ (*shouting*)   Chag Sameach! Chag Sameach! [*Good holiday.*] Now – please welcome our special guests for this Chanukah Par-tay! (*General hoots and screams.*) They are not from the Gaza Strip. They are not from East Jerusalem! And they are not from the West Bank! They – are – from – the Philippines! And they are – the Paper Dolls!!

Music of Bananarama: 'Venus'.

Three of the **Paper Dolls** (**Chiqui**, **Zhan**, **Jiorgio**) *appear onstage in costumes that look like amazing paper sculptures – woven, shredded, moulded. Home-made. Huge decorated headwear.*

They sing along with the instrumental track (heavy percussion) and dance with energetic, if somewhat derivative choreography borrowed from a wild mix of pop performance styles. The song is sweet and humorous and 'fabulous'.

Each **Doll** *has her own distinct style.*

Song: 'Venus' (in the style of Bananarama).

Verse 1 and Chorus.

Hot music vamps / underscores as **Chiqui** *takes centre stage with papier mâché crown and sceptre.*

Applause and hooting.

DJ (*reading*)   Here we have it, folks. Filipino royalty. The classiest queen in Tel Aviv, since Queen Esther put one over on Ah-hash'-ver-os'. Move over Sheba. Say hello to – Chiqui!

Paper Dolls (*taking up verse*)

Verse 2.

Zhan *takes centre stage in gown and boa.*

DJ Welcome Zhan, twenty-seven, who says she wants to follow in the footsteps of Lil' Kim, Christina Aguilera, and . . . Petula Clark! Yeah! And she's –

Paper Dolls (*singing*)

Chorus.

Musical underscore.

DJ And let's give a big Israeli welcome to – the sexiest doll to hit the streets! – Little bro – Jojo!

Jiorgio (*rapping under bridge, while other* **Dolls** *do 'back-up' vocals*)
  Don't be confused, 'cause they call me Jojo
  Try to read my 'paper', but that's a big no-no
  'Cause I know I got what you really really want
  Round the back – up the 'front'. (*Indicating his crotch.*)

Chiqui *registers disapproval.*

Chiqui *and* **Zhan**

Chorus.

Jiorgio (*solo*)

Chorus.

Chiqui *glares at* **Jiorgio** *as* **Cheska** *glides in with paper gown and mortarboard headpiece with sequins.*

DJ . Cheska is the newest Doll to hit Tel Aviv, her talent is fashion, and her goal in life is to – (*reading from a scrap of paper*) 'help the human race renew its passion for – education'. Our very own P–H–D. That stands for – 'P-P-P-P-Pilipino' Hot Drag!

Paper Dolls (*singing*)

Chorus.

Sally *appears behind them, body shielded by the others; all we see is her head poking up.*

DJ   Sally is thirty-eight. She has lived in Israel for seven years and wants to be a successful businesswoman one day. So . . . Martha Stewart and Oprah Winfrey – watch your backsides!

Suddenly and absurdly, the music switches gears. 'Venus' is overlaid with a new track: 'Tzena, Tzena'.

And **Sally** *is completely revealed. She wears a blue and white brassiere/bustier outfit made from newspaper and painted. (Think the Israeli flag in a 'D' cup, and bikini bottom.) Perhaps sheer harem pants over.*

Sally *is the soloist and launches into a famous Hebrew pop melody, 'Tzena, Tzena'.*

This drives the crowd wild. They sing along.

Sally
Song: 'Tzena, Tzena' (in the style of Connie Francis).

Verse 1.

Other **Dolls** *join in (and counterpoint with 'She's Got it', from 'Venus', etc.).*

Verse 2.

Chorus.

Sally *continues singing with* **Cheska**, **Chiqui** *and* **Zhan** *providing 'back-up'.*

Perhaps **Jiorgio** *is 'Moonwalking'.*

'Venus' mixes and melds with 'Tzena, Tzena', overlaid in untold ways. The number ends with a wild flourish and the crowd goes crazy.

DJ   Go! Go! Tzena girl! Get down on those soldiers! Yeah! And now, let's all dance, to a true Israeli hero – Dana International!

Sound: recording of 'Diva by Dana International.

A makeshift dressing area immediately after the performance.

The **Paper Dolls** *shuffle in and begin removing their costumes.*

Underneath the paper gowns are their 'tricks of the trade': strange underclothing that pads and shapes them – a bizarre collage of objects.

During the scene, **Zhan** *changes into a gown.* **Cheska** *and* **Sally** *change into street clothes.* **Jiorgio** *and* **Chiqui** *reapply make-up and primp. Barely contained pandemonium.*

Zhan (*to* **Jiorgio**)   Did you see that sexy one in front? With the black curly hair?

Jiorgio   Gaga [*stupid*] – they're Jewish. They all have black curly hair.

Zhan   No! The one standing next to Yossi.

Cheska   Who is Yossi?

Sally   Our number-one fan. Always with the camera.

Jiorgio   Yossi is the Paper Dolls' first groupie /

Zhan   Black curly hair makes me 'loka loka' [*crazy*] /

Jiorgio   He's probably straight. They're not all bakla [*gay*], / you know.

Zhan   Well, I think he was a gay.

Jiorgio   So what? You going to marry him? What about the guy last week?

Zhan   I have a very large heart.

Jiorgio   And he had a very large burat [*dick*].

Jiorgio *bites into a falafel.*

Cheska   What are you eating?

Jiorgio   Falafel.

Zhan   I do not know why you like this, Jojo. It's like eating sand. (*He grimaces.*)

Jiorgio   It is just bread and – what do they call this?

Zhan   I call it no taste.

Sally   Chickpeas.

Cheska   What is chickpeas?

Zhan   What we feed our goats back home.

Jiorgio   It is better than what Mrs Rosenberg cooks. She says she makes fish, but it looks nothing like a fish. Just a grey lump. And the house, it smells like something you cannot imagine. I think the old man has made, you know, in his pants.

Sally (*to* **Cheska**)   Gefilte fish. Do not listen to him, Cheska. There are many many good things in Tel Aviv.

Cheska (*proud in her costume*)   This I know – I could not do this at home. (*Indicating her dress and jewellery.*) And I never had such wonderful friends there.

Sally   Now you are here, Cheska, we are five. A real group. Am I right, Chiqui?

Chiqui *and* **Cheska** *hug.*

Chiqui   But you – Jiorgio! What did you do out there? (*He imitates his brother.*) 'I've got what you really really want? Round the back, up the front'?!

The others laugh.

Jiorgio (*defensive*)   Chiqui, this is my style!

Chiqui   I am the manager of the Paper Dolls, and we do it how we rehearse.

Jiorgio *shrugs.*

Chiqui   Help Zhan into her dress.

Chiqui *hands a slinky lamé gown to* **Jiorgio**.

Jiorgio (*holding up dress*)   She will need two of us and a quart of olive oil to squeeze into this! (*Holding dress out to* **Zhan**.)

Zhan (*grabbing dress*)   Puke mo! [*Your cunt!*]

Jiorgio   Chiqui, now that Cheska is here we can make more shows, better shows. Make money.

Sally   Yossi tells me he thinks we can be big stars in Tel Aviv.

Zhan   Yes. Famous. At the gay clubs.

Chiqui   If we are going to do this, we have to work very hard. Can you all rehearse on Sunday? After church?

Sally   I can. Chaim has a friend staying. So, he is okay without me / for a few hours.

Zhan   I will ask. On Sundays, the daughter is always around. And she won't stop kvetching on me. And she doesn't like to clean up the old man by herself.

Cheska   I will get my permission. I tell to Mrs Cohen – Sunday is my day to pray.

Chiqui (*to his brother*)   And you, Jiorgio?

Jiorgio (*looks around to everyone*)   Me? I am free. Like the wind.

Zhan (*grabbing* **Jiorgio** *and singing out*)   'And it seems to me that you live your life' –

Chiqui   Zhan!

Jiorgio *joins in singing with* **Zhan**, 'like a candle in the wind . . .'

Chiqui   Jiorgio! What do you mean you are free? Do you work Sunday or no?

Jiorgio   Maybe. Or maybe I will stop working there.

Cheska (*to* **Zhan**)   How can he just leave?

Sally   He cannot. Don't make jokes, Jojo.

Jiorgio   I tell you, that Mrs Rosenberg? I think she is a Jewish witch.

Chiqui   You try to be nice. You need this job! Don't act crazy.

Jiorgio   I am making some money – doing hairstyle. Maybe I do this full-time, no? I have talent / in that.

Zhan (*to* **Cheska**)   I don't like my job so much, but I would not think to leave.

Cheska   Jiorgio has Chiqui. If I had an older brother taking care / of me . . .

Jiorgio   No one takes care / of me!

Cheska   Jojo, you should be grateful for this job!

Everyone speaks at once.

Chiqui   No / one is leaving anything.

Zhan   He will end up in the prison.

Yossi *enters but no one sees him. He has a movie camera with him. He tries to get their attention, but cannot be heard above their talking.*

Yossi   Shalom? . . . Hello? . . .

Jiorgio   I am not afraid like you are. / Old 'Titas'.

Sally   Everyone, calm down. Do you want them to hear / us outside?

Chiqui (*starts to yell* – *in Tagalog*)   Hoy, mga bakla. Quiet na kayo. (*Indicating they will be overheard by audience next door. This in clear:*) We have a show to do.

Suddenly, they all see **Yossi** *and immediately stop arguing. Five drag queens in various stages of undress.*

Yossi   Hello?

Zhan (*covers herself with her dress, then sees it is* **Yossi**)   Yossi!

Yossi   Do you mind if – ?

They all surround **Yossi**.

Sally (*happy to see him*)   We see you – out there. Making your movie.

Jiorgio (*to* **Cheska**) Cheska, this handsome faygele – this is Yossi.

Yossi (*shaking* **Cheska***'s hand*)   Shalom.

Jiorgio (*imitating, making fun, in a sexy voice*)   'Sha-lo-o-om' . . .

Yossi (*ignoring* **Jiorgio**)   These guys, they expect you for weeks now.

Jiorgio (*running his hand through* **Yossi***'s hair*)   Yossi – I make for you a very nice 'blow dry'.

Chiqui   Jojo!

Sally (*to* **Cheska**)   Yossi makes movies. And he wants to make a movie of us. He knows important people in Tel Aviv. Right, Yossi? He promises to get us out of these smelly parties where they pay us nothing and to a big fancy club.

Chiqui   You have news from your Mr Nazari? He will come to see us?

Yossi (*looking around*)   So, this is your dressing place.

Yossi *picks up some article of underclothing – maybe tennis balls taped to an old bra.*

Yossi   What is this?

Zhan (*laughing*)   Cheska's 'bolero'.

Cheska   Those are my tits.

Zhan *and* **Jiorgio** *crack up.*

Yossi   Wow. So, this is where you make your magic, huh?

Zhan   Yes. Where little Jacob Libas, the boy from Manila, becomes – Zhan! (*He poses for* **Yossi**.)

Yossi (*looking through his camera lens and starting to film*)   Just – Zhan? Like – Madonna?

Zhan (*posing, enjoying the attention*)   No. Like – Cher!

Chiqui   Zhan, your song is coming soon.

Sally   Yossi, we think you forget about us.

Chiqui   And what about your promise – TLV Club?

Zhan (*trying to zip up tight gown; to* **Yossi**)   Here, help me.

Yossi (*stops filming; tries to zip up* **Zhan**)   Shit! I don't know how to do this. It is too small, no?

Sally *comes over to help. Together they barely zip it.*

Jiorgio   I told you it would take two people.

Zhan (*to* **Yossi**)   Yossi, you have a boyfriend? Maybe that curly hair boy in the front row?

Yossi   Amos! No! He's straight.

Jiorgio   I told you!

Yossi   He's a Rabbi – in Haifa.

Zhan   So – I could be a Rabbi's wife!

Sally   Not in Haifa.

Jiorgio (*coming on to* **Yossi**)   Yossi, you want to make a movie of me?

Chiqui   Jiorgio! Tama na 'yan! (*To* **Yossi**.) Do you have news for us about the TLV Club?

Yossi   I am trying. It takes time. (*Looking through his lens at the crazy undressed queens.*) Amazing. I always think I know everything there is to know about Israel, but the Paper Dolls, you are – something different. Sally – dance like on stage!

Sally *undulates in pantyhose with his taped stomach and* **Yossi** *films.*

Chiqui   I am not so sure we want for you to take these pictures. What do we get?

Yossi (*ignoring* **Chiqui***, to* **Cheska**)   Hold up your tits for me.

Cheska (*holding them to her chest*)   Yossi, what do you do when you are not flirting with Filipino drag queens?

Yossi   You see it. I make movies of life in Tel Aviv.

He pans the room, filming them.

I will make a documentary film, and so everyone will know the Paper Dolls.

Sally   Do not forget your promise, Yossi. That Mr Nazari will come to see us perform. Why does your friend not come?

Yossi   He is a very busy man. This is why I shoot this footage. To show him.

Jiorgio (*posing*)   Yes! Yes! Now we are five, we will be famous. (*Excited.*) I see a world tour like – the Spice Girls!

Cheska *and* **Zhan** (*together*)   Only pretty! (*They crack up.*)

Chiqui   You know, Yossi, we also are busy. Come to B'nei Brak, where we take care of our old men. We dress like boys, and the Jewish we take care of – *they* wear the costumes.

Zhan (*posing in her dress*)   But here – onstage – I am Sarit Hadad!

Cheska   Who is this?

Sally (*explaining to* **Cheska**)   Sarit Hadad. / She –

Yossi (*to* **Cheska**)   Sarit Hadad – the Celine Dion of the Holy Land.

Zhan (*she sings*)   'I'm not Madonna, not a primadonna. I'm not Christin-a, I've got no limousine-ah – ' (*He giggles.*) I know how to sing all of Sarit Hadad's songs. 'Today, Today' and 'A Little Crazy' . . . She is beautiful. If I ever have a lot of money, I want a face like Sarit Hadad.

Pauses while everyone takes this in.

Really!

Music begins here.

Zhan   Come watch me.

Zhan *tugs on* **Yossi** *and they go off.* **Jiorgio** *tries to leave as well.* **Chiqui** *pulls* **Jiorgio** *back.* **Sally** *remains with* **Chiqui** *and* **Jiorgio**.

DJ (*from off*)   Please welcome back, Miss – ZHAN!

We hear the crowd applaud, whistles. We see **Zhan** *upstage, back to us, in spotlight, and* **Yossi** *filming in the shadows of the club.* **Cheska** *watches from the dressing room for a few bars. Then cut to scene and music under.*

Zhan, *diva-like, with hand-held mic, sings to the crowd.*

Song: 'Ata Totach' ['You are a Cannon'] – in the style of Sarit Hadad.

First two lines of Verse 1 are heard, then song continues under following scene.

Chorus.

Music under.

Back in dressing room.

Cheska (*watching* **Zhan** *onstage*)   Zhan is very happy.

Chiqui   Jojo, make me a promise you do not do anything stupid.

Jiorgio   Chiqui. You are not Mama or Papa. (*Pause.*) Okay, I promise.

Sally   You need to listen to your brother, Jiorgio. Don't make trouble.

Jiorgio   Everything will be good, 'aunties' – you will see.

Cheska   Chiqui, do you think this Yossi is for real?

Chiqui   Who knows?

Sally (*who has changed into her street clothes*)   I live here seven years, Cheska. And what I learn? In Israel, nothing is exactly what you think.

Lights out on dressing room.

Zhan (*in spotlight, finishing song*)

Chorus (*final line*)*:* Atah ha'gadol me'kulam.

Applause.

Light shift.

Two weeks later.

Chaim*'s house.*

Chaim *is sitting in his easy chair to one side, reading a book. He has a bandage on his throat. He is reading.*

Sally, *casual in a woman's top and shorts and sandals, enters from kitchen with a small bowl.*

Sally   Papa, here. Sweet carrots. For you – while I finish making the dinner. I cooked them just a little. They are soft. Easy for you to swallow.

Sally *turns away and heads back to kitchen.*

Chaim *raps his fingers loudly on the table beside his chair. When he speaks, he occasionally coughs and cannot get words out. Sometimes he gives up and writes a note and* **Sally** *will read it aloud.*

Sally (*turning back*)   Just a minute, Papa. Let me take the food out, before it is dry. Then you will not be so happy with me.

Chaim (*rasps*)   Sally!

Sally   What is it?

Chaim   I am angry at you. This morning, when I was on the toilet. No paper! I called and called for you.

Sally (*remembering*)   Oh! Chaim, I thought you were asleep. I thought I had a little time to practise my song, so I had my music in my ears.

Chaim (*rasps*)   I do not pay you to sing.

Sally   Not yet! (*She laughs.*) Are you ready to eat?

Chaim *holds out a pad with a list on it.* **Sally** *takes it and reads from list.*

Sally   What? A shopping list? Now? (*He nods and she reads.*) 'Toilet paper, *TV Guide*, razor blades.' I have razor blades! Why don't you use mine?

Chaim *gives her a 'look' and then beckons* **Sally** *over. He picks up another book nearby, points to a page in this book.*

Chaim   Read for me. Your Hebrew!

Sally   Oy vey iz mir! The dinner will burn!

The phone rings.

(*To* **Chaim**.) Hold on, Papa. This will be your daughter. She said now she would call.

She picks up the telephone.

Hello!

She listens into the phone.

Ken. [*Yes.*] Shalom, Mrs Grossman. (*Pause.*) Adina.

She indicates to **Chaim** *that it is indeed his daughter, then listens to phone. Pause.*

Sally   Chaim is right here. He is happy you call. I am making a roast chicken for Shabbes. And basmati rice, the way he likes it. A pinch of cinnamon and raisins. And a salad. I keep him strong. (*To* **Chaim**.) Papa, Papa, it's your daughter.

Chaim *takes the phone, and listens as* **Sally** *goes to kitchen.*

Chaim (*on phone*)   Dan got', [*thank God*], as good as can be. You, Adina?

He listens a moment more, tries to talk, and then pounds on table, frustrated.

Sally *comes to him.* **Chaim** *hands phone back to* **Sally**, *and gestures for her to hold on a moment.*

Sally   Just a minute, Mrs Grossman. (*To* **Chaim**.) What, Papa? (*Into phone.*) He's writing something.

Chaim *writes on a notepad, hands it to* **Sally**, *and indicates that* **Sally** *should read his note to* **Adina**.

Sally (*into phone*)   Here, this is what he says. (*Reading.*) 'I am thrilled to take . . . parp.' (*Pause. Confidently rereading the note into phone.*) To take parp! (*Realising it makes no sense, she turns to* **Chaim**.) Parp?!

Chaim *gesticulates wildly at her and tries to speak but only a rasp comes out.*

Sally (*to* **Chaim**)   Well, you must print. Not this script! (*Into phone.*) I am learning to read my Hebrew but when he writes like this! (*She looks back at notepad.*) Ah! I see. Part! Take *part*. 'I'm thrilled to take *part* – (*pause*) in the medical study.'

She laughs, then a pause as she listens into phone.

Yes, I will take him myself, like always. And I will wait for him.

Pause.

Sally (*lowering her voice so* **Chaim** *does not hear*)   No, Mrs Grossman, I would not say he is failing – but for – his voice. Sometimes he cannot speak. Even to me, he writes things.

Pause.

This is true?! This would be very good. I know it would make him very happy.

Pause.

Chaim? Here, Adina has news for you.

She extends receiver to **Chaim** *who takes it and listens.*

Chaim (*into phone*)   Yes. (*Pause.*) When, Adina? (*Pause.*) Yes, it is time.

Then **Chaim** *makes a rasping sound, but nothing comes out. Frustrated, he bangs on table, hands phone to* **Sally**, *points to his throat.*

Sally (*taking the phone*)   He is tired, Mrs Grossman.

She watches him nodding his head, and then **Chaim** *mouths the words:* *'Shabbat Shalom'.*

Sally   He says: 'Shabbat Shalom'. And do not worry.

She hangs up phone.

Papa, Adina tells to you – she at last, comes to visit? Soon, yes?

Chaim *holds up one finger.*

Sally   At one month? This is good news. I want to meet your daughter. Now, at last, I will have some help.

Chaim *scribbles something and hands it to* **Sally** *who reads the note.*

Sally *(reading)*   'I want razor blades for *men*. I do not want to use your pink ones.' *(She laughs.)* What? You are afraid where my razor blades have been?!

He makes a face.

Adina and me, we will take you to visit the places you want. She and I, we can make plans.

Chaim   'A mensch tracht, und Gott lacht.'

Sally   What means this, Chaim?

Chaim   A person, he plans – and God, he laughs.

Sally   Papa, I am thinking, one day, you will come and see me perform, yes?

Chaim   I do not go to see pornography.

Sally *(laughs)*   Ai! Drag is not pornography! No, it is like . . . *(She thinks.)* You have never dressed up, in a costume, Papa?

Chaim *writes a note.*

Sally *(reading* **Chaim***'s note)*   'Once. When I was a young man, in teacher's college, at Purim.' *(To* **Chaim***.)* As what?

Chaim *(matter-of-fact)*   Queen Esther.

Sally   Queen Esther?! Really?! I see, Papa. So, you were a drag queen long before me!

She laughs and **Chaim** *waves her off.*

Lights down on **Chaim**'*s house.*

Sound: Cyndi Lauper's 'Girls Just Want to Have Fun'.

One week later.

Chiqui *is pushing* **Yaakov**, *an elderly Chasid, in a wheelchair.*

A small boombox is in a pocket at the back of the wheelchair, playing Cyndi Lauper.

Yaakov *is falling asleep.*

Chiqui (*rousing him*)   Yaakov, stay awake. It is not time to nap. Look at the children playing over there. How about we play our game? Keep our minds sharp. Yes?

Yaakov *nods.* **Chiqui** *looks around towards the children.*

Chiqui   I spy – with my little eye – something that begins with – 'G'. (*Looking towards the children.*)

Yaakov (*considering this*)   G.

Pause. **Chiqui** *nods.* **Yaakov** *thinks, points in distance.*

Yaakov   Goat.

Chiqui (*annoyed*)   Where is there a goat? That is cheating. There is no goat.

Yaakov (*bored, points in another direction*)   Tree.

Chiqui   Not 'T'. I said 'G'.

Yaakov   Juice!

Chiqui   Now you make jokes.

Yaakov (*insistent*)   Juice! Juice!

Chiqui   No, Yaakov. Juice starts with 'J', not a 'G'.

Yaakov   No. Juice! I'm tirsty. I vant my juice.

Chiqui (*stops wheeling the chair*)   In a minute, Papa. First show me a 'G'. (*Practically pointing at the children playing.*)

Pause.

Yaakov *looks around, then he looks up to the sky and points his cane.*

Yaakov (*pointing*)   G.

Chiqui (*looking up*)   G? Where is this G? In the sky? What, now you see a goose?

Yaakov (*defiant, pointing*)   No. (*Looks to* **Chiqui**, *matter-of-fact.*) God.

Chiqui *smiles, hugs him, hands him his sippy cup.*

Then **Chiqui** *turns music up.*

Yaakov *sings along with Cyndi Lauper.*

Yaakov (*as* **Chiqui** *wheels him off*)   Dey just vanna, dey just vanna – ah – ah. Dey just vanna. Girls just vanna have fun.

Lights shift.

Two weeks later.

Chiqui'*s apartment, in old Yemenite section of Tel Aviv.*

Cindy Lauper continues under on boombox.

Cheska, **Sally**, **Zhan** and **Jiorgio** *sitting together on a large mattress. All but* **Jiorgio** *are making paper dresses and rocking to the music on the boombox.* **Jiorgio** *is styling an 'Afro' wig on a Styrofoam head.*

Many plates of food all around. Massive amounts of newspaper are piled in front of them.

Sally   You see, Cheska? I use – (*holding up a newspaper*) *Haaretz* for the weaving. It is a stronger newspaper.

Zhan   I always use *Maariv*. Because there are more pictures and advertisements, and so you don't have to spend all that time painting after.

Sally   If you want colour, use *The Gay Paper*. We should support *The Gay Paper*.

Jiorgio   *The Gay Paper* is free. How are you supporting it? By tearing it into pieces?

Sally   Zhan says he wants colour! *The Gay Paper* is pink!

Zhan (*rolling his eyes*)   I don't want it to be *all* pink!!

Sally (*in Tagalog*)   Manash! Bulag ka nga. [*Girlfriend! You are blind!*]

Zhan   I will sit on your face!

Sally (*turns to* **Cheska**)   Cheska, save this paper for me. I will bring *Jerusalem Post* home for Chaim. He likes to read this.

Cheska   You are lucky to live in Chaim's house. The bus, it takes me an hour to get to my employer.

Zhan   No, you are the lucky one. My amo [*employer*] treat me like alipin [*slave*]. I work every hour every day.

Cheska   What do you think, Jojo?

Jiorgio (*changing subject*)   You know – I speak to Yossi last night.

Sally   *You* speak to him, Jojo? / Why?

Jiorgio   I tell to Yossi he should come to the Miss Israel Philippine Beauty Pageant and bring Mr Nazari to see us. This is a good idea, no?

They all agree excitedly.

Cheska   Ay! I broke my nail!

Zhan (*claps*)   Award! (*Tagalog expression.*)

Cheska   Look. Sally, will you make my nails later?

Zhan   Sally is the queen of the nails. This is how she catches her men!

Cheska   Her men! You have someone, Sally?

Sally   No, not now. A long time before –

Zhan (*interrupting, to* **Cheska**)   She was in love. With Ahmad. Oooh, so hot! An Arab.

Sally   Yes. A taxi driver in Tel Aviv.

Cheska   Where did you meet?

Zhan (*interrupting*)   In his taxi.

Sally *gives* **Zhan** *an annoyed look.*

Sally   In his taxi. I see he looks at me in his mirror. Then, he asks me out.

Cheska   And you go?

Sally   Of course. Should I deprive him of 'this'?

She laughs.

Zhan   Then one day he says to Sally: 'Are you ready?'

Cheska   Ready? For what? (*Pause.*) You mean . . .

Sally   He didn't know. He thinks I am a girl. So, at last, I cannot hide it any more. I say to him: 'Ahmad, listen, I have a big secret.' And I tell to him the truth.

Cheska   And so?

Sally   And so, we dated for four wonderful years.

Zhan   But in the end, Ahmad married an Arab woman. His people, they make him.

Sally   I cry and I cry. (*Pause.*) But, you know, life is short! And Chaim always tells to me, 'Lichyot et Harega'. Live for today!

Zhan (*looking at the newspaper he is holding*)   Sally! Cheska! Look! This photo! Do you see what it says here? Read.

Sally (*looking over* **Zhan**'s *shoulder, reading headline*) 'A city for illegal migrant workers to be built near Ben Gurion Airport.'

Zhan   It is a tent city. Can you imagine that? Here! Look at the photo. (*Pointing.*) It's like the house where the German people took all the Jewish! (**Zhan** *points and shows* **Sally**.) It's the same. Surrounded by electric fence.

They all gather round to see it, except for **Jiorgio**.

Cheska   The Immigration Police – they are everywhere now.

Zhan   With their blue flashing lights. Like space people.

Cheska   You think this thing, this is for real?

Sally   I do not know. Let us hope they will be better than this.

Chiqui *enters from outside. He is upset.*

Chiqui   Jiorgio, are you crazy? (*To the others, beside himself.*) Do you know what my stupid brother did? (*A pause.*) He quit his job.

Cheska *and* **Zhan** *look at each other.*

Sally *goes to* **Jiorgio**, *who moves off to the side.*

Sally   This is true, Jiorgio?

Zhan   Once a crazy bakla, always a crazy bakla.

Jiorgio (*to* **Chiqui**)   Who told you?

Chiqui   Do you think I would not find out!? Mrs Rosenberg, she will report you now to the agency. And how will you make money?

Jiorgio   That Mrs Rosenberg, she is a bru-ha [*witch*]. And always with the stinky breath. I don't care. I will make money, cutting hair.

Chiqui   Where, in the jail? You cannot do whatever you want. I will go speak to them, make it better.

Jiorgio   No! I am not going back there. My Jews were mean. Not like your family. Always shouting. I cannot do the things they ask, Chiqui. It is not for me. They did not accept me.

Chiqui   Go back and apologise / to them.

Jiorgio   I / will not.

Chiqui   I / promised Mama, that I will watch out for you but you make it impossible / for me.

Jiorgio   I did not ask to come here, Chiqui. You know this. You are the oldest and you are the one who make Papa so mad. So you leave, and I am the little one, so he hits me. Another bakla son.

Sally   Jiorgio, you have responsibility. (*Goes to him.*) You think I take care of Chaim, and do not feel bad about my nanay back home? She is sick. But here I make money to send, so she can buy the medicine.

Zhan   I send five hundred every month to my brother. My nephew, Nicasio? He can go to school on this. And he will not have to do what I do.

Jiorgio   You send your money to the people who do not even like you.

Sally (*stern*)   They are still family, Jiorgio.

Chiqui   Sally, talk to him. I am sick with this.

Jiorgio   What about Yossi? He will make us famous. We can sing and make / money.

Chiqui (*beside himself*)   Jojo!

Sally   Chiqui, eat something. Puchero? I make / you.

Jiorgio   I can cut hair, Chiqui. I have talent in this.

Chiqui   You have talent for making trouble. (*To* **Cheska**.) Last month, did you know? He 'fell in love' with a Turkish / guy.

Sally *and* **Zhan** *roll their eyes – they've heard the story.*

Jiorgio Chiqui –

Chiqui With a Turkish guy who takes his money. His things. Everything.

Jiorgio He didn't take. I gave / to him.

Chiqui And what do you have that you can give away? It is time for you to grow up. Sex is not everything. (*To* **Cheska**.) Back in the Philippines, he got beat up one time.

Jiorgio Tumahimik ka [*shut up*], / Chiqui! I promise to everyone, I will be careful.

Chiqui You and me Jojo, we will talk more later.

A moment.

Cheska (*trying to change subject*)   Chiqui, Yossi says that he will bring Mr Nazari to the Miss Philippine Beauty Pageant next week.

Chiqui Who tells to you this?

Zhan (*pointing at* **Jiorgio**)   Jiorgio –

All other **Dolls** *look to* **Zhan** *as if to say 'Shhh.'*

Sally Yossi calls me.

Chiqui And he says this Nazari comes to see us at the Beauty Pageant?

Sally *nods.*

Chiqui At least some good news today. Really? At last! So now, we must practise extra hard. (*To* **Jiorgio**.) So, Jojo, what song will you do at the Pageant?

Jiorgio A surprise!

Chiqui (*losing it*)   No more surprises from you! I make the programme! You know how it goes – the personality competition. Then, each of us will sing one song. The end.

Jiorgio Don't you trust me, Chiqui?

Chiqui (*in Tagalog*)   Puta ka, Jojo, pag hiniya mo ko, lagot ka sa kin. [*If you do anything to embarrass me, Jojo, you will be very sorry.*]

Chiqui *leaves.*

Jiorgio   You know, he only pretends to be a prude.

Sally   Jojo, your brother, she loves you very much, yes?

Jiorgio (*changing subject*)   Sally, let me do your hair for the Pageant.

Jiorgio (*dancing around* **Sally**, *playing with her hair, sings / raps*)
Sad girl, sad girl I'm such a dirty, bad girl
Toot toot uh, Beep, beep, uh
You bad girl, you sad girl
I'm such a dirty, bad girl
Toot toot, uh Beep, beep, uh –

Sally   Jojo, you give me a 'hair-ache'.

Jiorgio (*running his fingers through* **Sally**'s *hair*)   Wait! Do not move! I got it! Sally, you want – I make for you – a windswept bouffant 'up-do' or . . . maybe – or . . . (*He looks over at the wig.*) Maybe . . . if you like – A 'Jew-fro'!

Jiorgio *puts the Afro wig on* **Sally**'s *head.*

Jiorgio   Oooh – Miss Ross!

All Dolls (*together*)   Stop! In the name of love!

They all 'vogue' and then fall out.

Lights shift.

Transition: the **Chasid Chorus** *sing the prayer 'L'Cha Dodi'* (*Welcome the Sabbath Bride*).

Three weeks later. **Chaim**'s *house.*

The table is set with two candlesticks, unlit.

Adina, **Chaim**'s *daughter, stands near the table, nervous.* **Sally** *enters with challah bread on a platter.* **Adina** *notices* **Sally**'s *hot red painted nails.*

Sally (*places platter on table*)   There!

Adina   Salvador! Your nails!

Sally (*delighted, showing them off*)   You like, Mrs Grossman? It is called 'Red Sea'! But, I have a hundred different. 'Persian Pink', 'Milk and Honey'. If you want, I can make for you a manicure.

Adina   No, that's very nice, but –

Sally   I have lot of experience. Four friends. Eight hands. That's forty fingers a week! And then – the feets! Don't ask!

Chaim (*coming into the room*)   Sally! Adina! It is time. Shabbis!

Adina (*trying to make conversation*)   I must say – you set a beautiful table – Salvador.

Sally   Thank you, Mrs Grossman.

Adina   Salvador –

Sally   Please – Sally.

Adina (*takes a breath*)   Sally. I must confess – you are not – what I expect.

Sally   I am afraid Chaim did not expect it either. You remember, Chaim? You opened the door that first day? And – the look on your face! (*She laughs.*) The first thing Chaim says to me: (*Imitating a serious* **Chaim**.) 'I asked for a man.' I say: 'But I *am* a man!'

Chaim *chuckles at the memory.*

Sally (*to* **Adina**)   I tell to him: 'If you hire me, you will see how hard I work. And if you do not, you will *not* see how hard I work.' (*She turns back to* **Chaim**.) Seven years I live here, Papa.

Chaim (*to* **Adina**)   He took some getting used to.

Sally (*to* **Adina**)   And you think *he* did not?

Chaim *and* **Sally** *share a look.*

Chaim   Candles.

Sally *and* **Adina** *stand at the same time. An awkward moment.*

Adina   Oh, I see. No, please, you go ahead. I have not said the blessings in a very long time.

Sally *takes a napkin from the table and places it on her head. She circles her hands around the flames three times.*

Sally (*chants, slowly*)   Baruch atah adonai elohainu melech ha-olam, asher kid-shanu, b-mitzvah tav, vitzi-vanu, l-hadlik ne'er shel Shabbat.

Chaim, Sally *and* **Adina**   O-mehyn. [*Amen.*]

Chaim (*beaming*)   She is good, no?

Adina (*stunned, just begins to express her feelings*)   I am – very impressed. A regular Yentl, this one.

Sally (*beams proudly*)   I will check on dinner.

She leaves for the kitchen.

Adina (*suddenly she can speak her mind*)   Papa, this is all a bit crazy, no? Do you not see it is odd? Listen to me. Today, your neighbour, Mrs Stein, she tells me that one night she sees this 'Sally' on a bus. (*With emphasis as if to shock* **Chaim**.) In a dress. And high heels. (*Loud whisper.*) Like a zonah [*whore*]!

Chaim   Vos viylstu, Adina? [*What do you want, Adina?*] This is life in Tel Aviv for an old man, who lives alone.

Adina   No, Papa. (*Pause.*) I have been thinking. I have been enough time apart from you. (*Pause.*) What I want, Abba, what I want – (*she hesitates*) is to bring you back with me to New York. To live.

Chaim   A crazy idea, Adina. Why now?

Adina   Because it is time. I want you with me.

Chaim   Too late for this!

Adina   After everything we have been through, we need to be together. A family.

Chaim   So? You come back to Israel.

Adina   Papa, you know better.

Chaim   I am comfortable, Adina. (*He looks towards the kitchen.*) And what will become of Sally?

Adina   Sally? Sally will find another job!

Chaim *shakes his head.*

Adina   Tel Aviv is still not safe for you. A bomb every other week! We read in the papers. Last week on that bus. All those people. How do I know you are not there?

Chaim *waves her off.*

Adina   Daddy −

Sally *brings in the food and sets it down.*

Sally   I hope you will enjoy. Chaim, he likes the meat with the sweet apples and apricots.

Adina   You make a tsimmes?! She's a real ballabustah, Daddy. (*To* **Sally**.) What do you think, Sally? I want for Chaim to come with me back to America.

Chaim   Adina!

Sally (*shocked*)   You mean − to visit in New York? Yes −

Adina   I mean − to live with me. From now on. Don't you think that's best?

Sally (*flustered, but trying to hide it*)   Oh, of course. It − it is always best for a family to be together. Me, I also miss my mother. I wish to be there but I work here and send money home to her.

Adina   See, Abba? Sally wants what is best, too.

Chaim (*bangs on table, angry, rasping*)   I will make this decision. (*Pointing.*) Not you – or you. I have lived in Israel almost all my life. I fought in the Hagganah to make this country. I will not leave it. I will die – here.

Adina   Be reasonable Papa. Think. What will happen if you get sick again –

Chaim (*rasps*)   I will be fine.

Adina   You will not be fine.

Chaim   No, Adina! No more talk. Genug! [*Enough!*] It is Shabbes. The Kiddush.

Sally   Papa, talk to your daughter.

Adina (*furious*)   And why this one! – She calls you Papa?!

Sally (*to* **Adina**)   I do not mean . . . It is only for respect. (*To* **Chaim**.) Chaim – your daughter has come a long way. You need time together. I am not hungry tonight.

Chaim (*rasps*)   Kiddush. Sally will speak for me.

He gives wine glass to **Sally**.

Sally *looks at* **Adina** *uncomfortably. Stands, uneasy, picks up her wine glass.*

Sally (*tentatively, chants*) Baruch atah adonai elohainu melech ha-alom, bo'rye – (*She stops.*)

Chaim (*finishing for her*)   Bo'ray? (*Urging her on.*)

Sally   Bo'ray Pree – Hagafen.

Chaim   O-mehyn.

Chaim *crosses to* **Adina**.

Adina (*looks up at him*)   Abba.

Chaim (*taking* **Adina**'s *face in his hands*)   Adina, yal-da sheli [*my little girl*]. It makes my heart happy – to have you here with me.

He kisses **Adina**'s *forehead, then turns to* **Sally**.

Chaim   And Sally. One thing. For me – I ask now a small favour. (*He glances over at* **Adina**.) When you go outside, on the street, no more dressing – like a woman. You understand?

Two weeks later.

Transition: Miss Philippine Israel Beauty Pageant.

Light shift. Unfurling of Israeli flag.

A beat.

Transition: the five **Paper Dolls** *sing Israel's National Anthem, 'Hatikva'.* **Yossi** *off to side filming.*

Lights only on faces reveal **Zhan**, **Cheska**, **Jiorgio** *standing side by side in 'swimwear', some holding tiny Israeli flags. Hands to their chests, join in singing the second verse of 'Hatikva'.*

Od lo avda tikvatenu,
Hatikva bat sh'not alpayim,
Lihyot am chofshi be'artzenu
Eretz Tziyon virushalayim.

Lihyot am chofshi be'artzenu
Eretz Tziyon virushalayim.

Beauty Pageant Announcer (*stands with mic*)   You have seen the personality interviews. And now – the final chapter of our Beauty Pageant – the talent competition. Please welcome our first talent contestant– Jiorgio Val Paraiso!

Jiorgio *steps forward.*

Cheska, **Zhan** *and* **Chiqui** *stand to one side. They are* **Jiorgio**'s *'back-up' singers.* **Sally** *enters, running late, and joins them.*

Song: 'This is My Life' (in the style of Shirley Bassey).

Jiorgio

Verse 1.

Jiorgio *pulls off his giant hat and shakes out his long silky black hair. Music builds to dramatic finish.*

*Chorus (other **Dolls** sing back-up, in Hebrew).*

*Chorus repeats (other **Dolls** sing back-up).*

Before final two repeats of last line, **Jiorgio** *tears off his gown to reveal a skimpy bra, pantyhose with huge dildo attached to the front.*

Cheska, **Sally**, **Zhan** *are aghast.* **Zhan** *covers his mouth to hide his laughter.* **Chiqui** *stomps offstage, furious.*

Jiorgio
  This – is – my – life!!

He collapses on stage dramatically.

Beauty Pageant Announcer (*panicked*)   Wasn't that – charming!? And now, for a change of pace, please welcome our next contestant, Chiqui Val Paraiso, singing 'To Sir, with Love'.

Light shift.

Music: intro to 'To Sir with Love'. Immediately –

Backstage dressing area.

Zhan, **Cheska** *and* **Sally** *enter with* **Jiorgio**, *who holds the dildo proudly in his hand,* **Yossi** *right behind them, filming.*

Zhan (*grabbing dildo*)   Ai, Bakla, here did you get it?

Jiorgio   From Yossi's car.

Jiorgio *and* **Zhan** *howl.*

Yossi   Very funny.

Cheska (*to* **Jiorgio**)   Why you make all the attention on you? We are supposed to be together, Jojo.

Sally   Jojo, what do you think your brother will say about this? And in front of Mr Nazari? It is not proper.

Jiorgio *takes the dildo and goes to* **Sally**, *waving it at her.*

Jiorgio   Whatever you say, *Imelda.*

Zhan *laughs.*

Sally   You can all make jokes but you embarrass us in front of Mr Nazari.

Jiorgio   Yossi, you think I will win the judges? *You* think I am sexy, no?

Zhan (*to* **Jiorgio**)   Yossi wants a real man. I tell you, we are not his type.

Jiorgio   I think Yossi *likes* 'Orientals'. (*Egging him on.*) What do they call that, Yossi?

Zhan   A rice queen!

Jiorgio   Are you a rice queen, Yossi?

Yossi (*puts camera down*)   I am not any kind of queen. You want the truth? Shaving my entire body and all, like you do? It would make me feel – ashamed.

Zhan   Me? I would be ashamed to be like you. Monkey hair – all over!

Jiorgio *and* **Cheska** *fall out, laughing.*

Chiqui *enters, hysterical.*

Chiqui   You have made a big disaster! I could not even finish my song!

Zhan, **Chiqui** *and* **Cheska** *in shock.*

Jiorgio (*to* **Chiqui**)   And the best actress goes to –

Zhan *giggles.*

Chiqui   I know you think it is funny. But this is not what we do. The judges may disqualify all of us! You only bring more attention on yourself. And in your situation –

Jiorgio   You are only jealous.

Chiqui (*in* **Jiorgio**'s *face*)   Mamaya na. Yoko sa harap ng iba. [*Later. I don't want to talk in front of other people.*]

Jiorgio   Don't talk to me like this, Chiqui! I am not a child.

Chiqui   Ha? Para kang baby. [*You – are like a baby!*]

Jiorgio   You act like an / old man.

Chiqui (*crossing to* **Yossi**)   And what did you think of this 'performance' of my stupid brother?

Yossi *glances uneasily at* **Jiorgio**.

Yossi   Honestly? I think Jiorgio's song is funny. Everyone laughed.

Chiqui (*grabbing the dildo*)   And this is what you put in your movie? Maybe this is what you think we do for TLV club? Tell me, did your friend, Mr Nazari, like this show of my brother?

Yossi (*pause*)   Nazari, he – he did not come today. I am sorry.

The **Dolls** *react to this.*

Chiqui (*after a beat*)   Maybe, this is just as should be.

Sally   You make us a promise, Yossi. That Mr Nazari comes to see us.

Jiorgio   Who cares? Yossi likes me.

Yossi *starts filming him.*

Jiorgio   I know the judges they like me. I will win. I mean, who else? Nobody else. (*To* **Yossi**.) I am the sexiest. (*Goes to* **Sally**.) Sally has got nice tits. But it's because of the hormones she used to take. They got big. That's all. And Zhan? Zhan you are very beautiful but you know – (*Pinches* **Zhan**'s *cheeks, makes a 'fat' gesture. To* **Cheska**.) Cheska – such a nice face but you are flat up here.

Chiqui   Jiorgio, when you are done telling the Mossad everything about your friends, you will come talk to me. Sally – get ready, you will go next. (*To* **Yossi**.) And you, Mr Schumann, I think maybe you are done now with your making your movie.

Chiqui *hands dildo to* **Jiorgio** *and walks out.*

Yossi   Chiqui. No. Wait.

Yossi *follows* **Chiqui** *out.*

Cheska (*to* **Jiorgio**)   You make it hard for us, Jojo. Please, come. Talk to your brother.

Cheska *pulls* **Jiorgio** *off.* **Sally** *and* **Zhan** *remain.* **Sally** *helps* **Zhan** *reapply make-up, fix her clothes etc.*

Zhan   They will make it up. They always do.

Sally (*occurring to her for first time*)   Do you think that Yossi ever really tells about us to this – 'Nazari'?

Zhan *shrugs his shoulders.*

Sally (*putting on* **Zhan**'s *eye make-up*)   Zhan, do you ever miss home?

Zhan   I do not think on it.

Sally   I miss the rain.

Zhan   The rain?! It always frizzed my hair.

Sally   I miss the smell of the wet. And the big Philippine rain. That went, how you say, sideways.

Zhan   Ay! The Hangin. That awful wind. It always blew my 'do'.

Sally   So, you do not miss anything?

Zhan *pauses.*

Zhan   When I am old. And I am rich. Then – I will go home. And I will build a big house in Cebu. And all my relatives will be jealous. And I will have a maid. And she will wait on me hand and foot! And my hair – it will always be – perfection!

We hear musical intro to Vicky Carr, 'It Must be Him'.

Light shift.

Three weeks later.

Friday afternoon. A street in the ultra Orthodox neighbourhood of Bnei Brak.

Chiqui and **Cheska** *outside the mikveh [bath house] each with their Chasid client.*

Cheska's *old man,* **Isaac**, *is in a wheelchair beside a bench.* **Chiqui** *is combing his* **Chasid**, **Yaakov**'s *hair gently.*

The **Dolls** *wear jeans.* **Jiorgio** *is nearby reading a magazine.* **Cheska** *kneels opposite the wheelchair doing exercises with a cane that* **Isaac** *and* **Cheska** *hold horizontally in their hands.*

Isaac *pushes the cane forward.*

Cheska (*to* **Isaac**)   Do it again. D'choff. D'choff. D'choff. [*Push. Push. Push.*]

Isaac feebly moves the cane.

Cheska   Very good! Again . . .

Isaac *stops exercis, reaches into his pocket and pulls out a yarmulke (kippah). He places it on* **Cheska**'s *head.* **Cheska** *awkwardly accepts it.*

Cheska (*to his* **Isaac**)   Yes, Isaac. Okay. (*To* **Chiqui**.) Do you see? He wants for me to be like him. Do you know what his son, my employer, wants me to do? (*Pointing to* **Isaac**, *who is staring, but not cogent.*) His son tells to me this week he will help me to stay here – if I wear the kippah. And – he wants for me to cut my hair. And also, remove the earrings. And wear the clothes they wear. Can you see me like a Chasid?

Chiqui   Better you become an Orthodox wife.

Jiorgio   I will shave your head for you!

Chiqui   Yes, and you can wear, what do they call it? A sheitel. Why do they do this? I mean, if you are going to wear a wig, why that rag?!

Jiorgio   Sometimes I think the little Chasid children, they cry so much because their mothers are so ugly!

Cheska   But, without this job, no visa. Overnight I would no longer be legal. It will take a year for me to pay back the agency – thirty-five hundred dollars.

Jiorgio   You do not have to do this. Look at me. I find something I like more.

Chiqui   And you have to hide away, like a rat.

Yossi *enters with* **Zhan** *who walks slowly with his* **Old Man**.

Zhan (*indicating* **Yossi**)   Look who I find! Cruising the Jewish ghetto!

Yossi (*to the* **Dolls**)   I came looking for you – and I come with happy news.

Zhan (*can't contain himself*)   Mr Nazari has agreed – for an audition!

Yossi   Zhan! Mr Nazari says he is very sorry he did not come to the Pageant, so he will make for you a special audition.

Zhan *sits with his* **Old Man**, *takes out yogurt and spoon, and feeds him slowly, like a baby.*

Jiorgio   This is true! When? When?

Yossi   He will make it in two weeks. This is good?

Zhan   Finally! Sarit Hadad – at TLV!

Chiqui (*going to* **Yossi**, *shakes his hand*)   But, Yossi, where do we make this audition? You must find for us a place. You know we rehearse at my flat but this is not right for him to come there.

Yossi   Now, you want for me to find a place?

Chiqui   You owe us this. So, it is up to you, Yossi. (*To other* **Dolls**.) Two weeks! I am – a little scared.

Cheska   I will get some dances ready to practise. And we sew new costumes.

Yossi   You will make it good, I know. (*Looks around.*) What is this place? A mikveh?

Jiorgio (*takes* **Yossi** *by the arm, pointing*)   Yes, the sacred bath house.

Chiqui   You know, Yossi, we used to peep at them making . . . you know, in the steam room.

Yossi   What do you mean?

Chiqui   There. In the mikveh, we climb up to the top of the window, and we see them. Nude. And some of them are making . . . you know – (*He makes a jerking-off motion.*)

Yossi   No!

Cheska   Really, really. Yes, two. Two men, they making . . .

Yossi   What, a hand job?

Zhan (*very excited*)   Yes, yes . . .

Yossi   Two old Chasids?

Zhan   No, no. They are young.

Chiqui   Yes, young. And handsome.

Yossi (*getting into fantasy*)   Really?

They walk towards the 'wall' of the mikveh.

Cheska   I'll show you. (*He points to a 'window' in the stone wall.*) We stand here and open the window a little. So we can see what's inside.

Chiqui   So many times they broke the glass. Without the glass, it's good for us. Because we don't need to open it, we just look and see, and we can see everything. Go. Go look. Make a movie.

Yossi   No, I don't think so!

Cheska   You are afraid of what? Just – take a peek.

Yossi *looks around to be sure no one is watching, hoists himself up and looks in.*

Cheska   What's happening?

Jiorgio   You see something?

Young Chasidic Man (*suddenly entering from upstage*)   Hey! Hey! What are you doing? Get down! What is going on? You! You!

Yossi *drops down.*

Yossi   I'm doing nothing. The window . . . it is broken. I was checking.

Young Chasidic Man   What? You are the glass-fitter? This is a holy place. What do you want? Who are you?

Yossi   Nobody. It is no big deal.

Young Chasidic Man   I can see what you are. Please go. Take your 'friends'. This is a place that belongs only to us! It's not your business. Go. Do not come back.

He leaves.

Yossi   You will get me into real trouble some day!

The **Paper Dolls** *laugh.*

Chiqui *and* **Zhan** *go back to the bench to their old men.*

Zhan   Do you know – these religious people think they're the only sons of God – they are the Chosen Ones.

The **Old Man** *pulls on* **Chiqui**.

Chiqui *takes out a comb and combs the* **Old Man**'s *beard.*

The **Old Man** *stares vacantly.*

Chiqui   He has Alzheimer's, so he forgets everything. Now, he even forgets his name and sometimes he doesn't know me. It makes me feel bad.

*The **Old Man** begins to try to speak. **Cheska** wipes his face, gives him a little water from a 'sippy cup' with a straw.*

Cheska   Do you want anything else? (*Kneeling to the **Old Man**.*) Do you need a tissue? I have one. (*Then **Cheska** realizes the chair is wet. To **Yossi**.*) Hand me a towel.

Yossi *gets the towel from back pocket of wheelchair.*

Cheska (*to **Yossi***) Here, can you help?

Yossi *helps **Cheska** raise the **Old Man** from his chair and stands with him. Then **Cheska** wipes down the soiled wheelchair.*

Yossi *is left alone with the **Old Man** for a moment.*

*The **Old Man** stares at **Yossi**, touches his cheek, as if to say 'Who is this?'*

Yossi (*uneasy*)   What does he want? (*Referring to **Old Man**.*)

Cheska (*talking to his **Old Man**, as he cleans chair*)   Hey! This is Mr Schumann. He is our friend. Don't worry. Don't be afraid.

*The **Old Man** speaks gibberish. Drools or spits up a bit. **Cheska** comes over and gently cleans him up, rubs his back and caresses his cheeks.*

Cheska   It's okay, Papa. We're going now.

*Slowly, lovingly, **Cheska** takes **Old Man** from **Yossi**, sits him carefully in the wheelchair.*

Zhan   Wait for us. We will come too. Bye-bye. Shalom, Yossi.

Zhan *gets his **Old Man** to stand.*

Chiqui   Yossi, time to get Papa home. A bath and bed. (*To **Yaakov**.*) Right Yaakov?

They all begin to leave.

Jiorgio (*to **Yossi***)   Where will you go for Shabbat? You have friends?

Yossi   Of course I have friends!

Yossi *stands, nowhere to go.* **Jiorgio** *lounges nearby.* **Zhan,**
Cheska *and* **Chiqui** *begin to leave.* **Chiqui** *walks with his arm*
firmly around **Yaakov***'s shoulder, then turns back.*

Chiqui   Yossi – my advice? Do not get caught peeping
again! You be a good Jewish boy, you hear?

Chiqui *glances over at* **Jiorgio***.*

Sound: many people reciting prayers.

Light shift.

One week later.

At the Kotel, the Western Wall.

A few men and women in Orthodox dress, praying.

Chaim *stands between* **Adina** *and* **Sally** *arm in arm, looking*
around. **Sally** *is transfixed by the scene in front of her. She is dressed in*
slacks and top, with a colourful shawl around her shoulders.

Sally   Finally, Papa, we are here. What you asked. (*She looks*
around.) This is how I imagined it. (*To* **Chaim**.) How you told
me it would be. Yerushalayim. The stones *are* like gold. And
see – over there. It looks like the whole Israeli army!

Adina (*with cynicism*)   They choose the handsomest men and
the most beautiful women to be here in Jerusalem – by the
Wall. This way, the tourists think the Israeli army is the sexiest
in the world, and so the Americans, they send more money.

Chaim   Sally, you write prayer on – piece paper, and you –
(*he mimes folding paper*) fold – and put into — holes in Kotel. (*He*
points.) Between the stones. They say, at night, God takes –
reads – and answers your prayer.

Sally   No Papa, I will not ask God for more. You keep on
asking, and soon God will tell you, 'You ask for something
every day! Enough, already, enough!' Shall we go, Chaim?

She begins to take **Chaim** *to the Wall. He stops her, and looks towards* **Adina***.*

Adina   Sally, you cannot go to the men's side, looking like this. They will stop you. Let him go by himself. Abba, go on. Make your prayers. I will wait here.

Chaim *walks off to the men's side.* **Sally** *is unsure what to do with herself.*

Adina (*looks around*)   Look at them – men on one side. Women on the other. Asking. Praying.

Sally   You know, Jerusalem is a holy city, but not just for the Jewish. For us, too.

Adina   Everyone comes to Jerusalem to talk to God. Better they buy a lottery ticket. (*Pause. Turns to* **Sally***.*) Sally, I need for you to help me. To make my father understand that it is a good thing for him to come back with me, to New York. If you act pleased about this, he will listen.

Sally   And you think it is the best for him? To leave what he knows?

Adina   Yes, of course. To be with family, at the end, this is what has to be. Chaim is all I have now, Sally. It is different for you.

Sally (*looks at her*)   Adina, you think that people like us do not want things? Like a family? When I was growing up in a small town in the Islands, do you think I plan to be a 'Paper Doll', in Israel? For now, the Paper Dolls are my family. And Chaim – he is my family, too. He is what I have.

Adina   You are paid to take care of Chaim. You have a job. And you do it very well. I know my father cares for you. But it is a job.

Sally   In Philippines, a family will have many childrens, and some will go away. But the mamas and the papas, we will not leave them with a stranger. Here in this holy land, why do the sons and the daughters leave?

Adina   It is not for you to judge me, Sally.

Sally   Why Chaim, who is old, must now go away to a new place he does not know? If you want for you and Chaim to be together, I do not understand why you do not come back to Israel.

Adina (*pause, looks around*)   Sally – my son, Ezra, he made Bar Mitzvah here, at the Wall.

Sally   Yes, I know. I have seen this photo.

Adina (*turns to* **Sally**)   So then, Chaim has told you – about Ezra.

Sally   Yes. And I am so sorry. I cannot begin to imagine.

Adina   No, you cannot. They tell me that with time, things change. But this is not true. I never can forget this day. A soldier comes to my door. 'Your son has died,' he says. I think: 'How is this? Where was there even fighting?! What, a suicide bomb?' Then I hear – 'mistake', 'accident'. 'What kind of accident? A car?' No. He calls it – 'friendly fire'. Such stupid words. My son, a soldier in the IDF, killed, by another Israeli! God makes such a 'mistake'.

Pause. They stare at the Wall.

Sally   Look at Abba. So small, standing. You know, Adina, Chaim is not a religious man. For seven years I am with him, Chaim does not ask to come to Jerusalem. I think now, he is here for you. He takes you here for a reason. He brings you here – so you will no more be afraid of this Wall.

Adina   What – Chaim tells this to you?

Sally *says nothing.*

Pause.

Adina   Sally, for me to stand at the Kotel is not going to change anything. It is not that simple. But if *you* believe, Sally, go. Go to the Wall. Make your prayers.

Sally *looks at* **Adina** *and then starts towards the women's side. And then she turns back.*

Adina   What is it? Why do you stop?

Sally   I do not know where I go. Which side? (*She looks at* **Adina**, *a bit stricken.*) I may look like I *am*, but, you know, Adina, you understand, I am not.

Adina   I do not understand you Sally. I do not understand – anything about you. But you say you believe in God, so does it matter at which side of the wall you pray? (*Slight pause.*) Or maybe you feel ashamed, in front of God?

Sally *looks from* **Adina** *to the Wall. The women stand, side by side, not moving, in the golden light of Jerusalem.*

Light shift.

Chasid Chorus *sing a slow, beautiful version of the prayer 'Oseh Shalom'.*

One week later.

House of **Yossi**'s *mother*, **Yael**. *Lights up on her living room/kitchen.*

Jiorgio, **Zhan** *and* **Cheska** *stand with lots of shoulder bags and rolling suitcases. They look around.* **Yael** *stands, smiling and perplexed.*

Yossi *enters with* **Chiqui**. *He has armfuls of costumes and carries a huge boombox, which he sets down.*

Yossi   C'mon. I'd like you to meet my mother. Don't be shy. (*To* **Yael**, *who is holding a big plate of babka.*) This is Chiqui.

Chiqui   Shalom.

Yossi   And his brother, Jiorgio. And this is / Zhan. And Cheska –

General hellos, shaloms, etc.

Yael (*obviously uncomfortable*)   I'll forget names by / tomorrow.

Sally *enters last.*

Yossi   – Cheska. And this – is Sally.

Yael's *friend,* **Ester**, *an Israeli woman in her forties, enters with more food on a plate.*

Ester   Shalom everyone! I bring you some chopped herring, some kishka. Help yourselves. / I made it.

Yael   This is my friend, Ester. She is your audience / tonight.

Ester   Eat. Eat. It's very good. (*Shoving food at them but their hands are full.*) Take! *This* is chopped herring. You like? Me, I like creamed – but some people, they cannot digest, so I don't know, so I make with vinegar, / sugar.

Yael   Ester, give them a minute. They just got here. Their hands are full, don't / you see?

Yossi   I told you not to make a fuss.

Yael (*to the* **Dolls**)   Please put your things down, make yourself at home. We are haimish [*homey, cosy*].

Ester (*to* **Cheska**)   And this, this is kishka. You know from kishka? It is intestines, but you do not have to tell this to anyone. It's good. Come, try!

Yael (*to* **Yossi** *but a bit loud*)   What are they? (*Then, to the* **Dolls**.) I am his mother. He was in my stomach. I love him / very much.

She grabs **Yossi** *by the cheeks.*

Yossi   Mom, don't start. You're embarrassing me. (*To* **Ester**.) And I said, do not / make –

Ester   It's nothing. You know I love to cook. And it's for your girlfriends. (*Up to sky, to God.*) Finally he brings home some girlfriends. (*She pinches* **Yossi**'s *face.*)

Yael *nudges her to be quiet.*

Yael (*to* **Ester**)   Shah!

Ester   What? What did I say?

Yael (*shaking her head 'no'*)   The 'girls', the '*girls*', will eat later, Ester. After their show.

She gives **Ester** *a 'look'.*

Ester (*dawns on her that they are not girls*)   Azoy! [*Really!*]

Yael (*to* **Sally**)   I have five boys – like a basketball team, like the five books of Moses, and still, I cry all day. You know why? Three children are in America. And another one, he travels to India to how you say, 'find himself'. In my kitchen, I have three clocks on the wall. One. Two. Three. Each a different time. One is New York City. One is Portland. And Dallas. I am fed up with their being away. I do not even know my grandchildren. They were here once in the last five years. They don't know their grandmother.

Yossi   Mom, okay . . .

Sally   You really cry every day?

Yael   Every day. All the time. I make myself meshugah from it. You know what this means?

Yossi   My mother means / she goes crazy.

Sally   I know from 'meshugah'. Chaim makes me / so –

Chiqui   My family in the Philippines is ten. Four boys. And six girls.

Yael   Ten! And your mother is not crazy?

Ester (*pointing at* **Chiqui**)   You look like a woman.

Chiqui   Thank you.

Ester   I think – I am a woman, and yet, I do everything a man does, but I don't want to *be* a man.

Chiqui   Since I was little, I have a dream. That I wish I was a 'her'. I wish I was a woman with a husband and children. Sometimes I fantasise. We all have dreams, you know?

Yael   I only have one dream. My dream is that my whole family is back together again, here in Israel.

Chiqui   I have that same dream. I do. That I make enough money to bring my family together.

Yossi   Enough talk for now. Nazari. He has to be impressed. If he will like you tonight, he will take you to the TLV. Go and get ready. The bedroom. (*He points.*)

Cheska (*to* **Jiorgio**)   I hope Mr Nazari shows up.

Zhan   Yossi, you are our hero.

The **Paper Dolls** *shuffle out to the bedroom to change.*

Yael   Some hero. A regular Moyshe Dayan. Right, Ester?

Ester (*exiting to kitchen with food*)   Don't ask me. I'm oysgemu'chet [*tired from excitement*].

Yossi   Nazari must like them. And, you cannot believe the movie I am making of this. It is crazy.

Yael   And what will you do with this movie?

Yossi   A film festival. If I finish soon. Nazari, he knows people. He is going to show the film to a producer in Jerusalem. And this producer has a friend in Los Angeles.

Yael   Los Angeles! My son, the macher [*big shot*]! What next? And then you are done with them?

Yossi   Done?

Yael   You will show your movie and people see them and will think – what? That you make fun – they are freaks?

Yossi   Of course not.

Yael   Yosseleh, do you even know these – men? How they feel?

Yossi   About what?

Yael   Are they afraid?

Yossi   Afraid?

Yael   On the news – I hear the same reports that you do. The police are rounding up illegal workers?

Yossi   They are not illegal.

Yael   Are you sure you should be so involved?

Yossi   I am not 'involved'.

Yael   No, this is my point. You are not, and this is a problem. I see they trust you.

Yossi   Ema –

Yael   I know very little about your life, Yosseleh. Even if you share it with – a nice man.

Yossi *tries to speak.*

Yael   Which I pray you do. You tell nothing to your mother. Fine – it is your life. But these people you bring home to me – these 'Paper Dolls' – they are not for you to play with.

A loud knocking.

Nazari (*from outside, as he enters*)   Hello! Hello!

Yossi   Nazari!

Nazari   Is this the place? Shalom!

Yossi   Shalom.

Nazari *enters. He is thirty-something, baseball cap, five-o'clock shadow. Handsome, wiry frame, fashionable tight jeans. A bit 'euro-trash'.*

Yossi (*greeting him*)   This is my mother. Her friend. (*Awkward pause.*) You made it!

Nazari   Of course. Why not? You promise me – something very special. So I am here. But I do not have a lot of time. TLV Club will be double-crowded tonight. These 'dolls' of yours? They are here?

Yossi   You will now see for yourself.

Nazari   So – let's get started!

Yossi   Sit. Sit. I will get them.

He exits to bedroom. **Nazari** *is left alone with* **Yael.** *Awkward pause.*

Ester (*holding out plates*)   Herring? Kishka?

Nazari *shakes his head.*

Yael   Something to drink maybe? A beer? Schnapps?

Nazari   A cold beer is good.

Ester (*trying to make conversation*)   Yossi tells us about your club −

Nazari   TLV.

Ester   It is a nice place? For dancing? I was quite a dancer in my day. Am I right, Yael?

Yael *rolls her eyes and serves a beer to* **Nazari**.

Yael   A regular Ginger Rogers.

Ester   And I bet you make fancy-schmanzy cocktails.

Nazari   Yes, we have a big bar. Everything. A deejay. And we have shows.

Ester   Yes? What kind of shows?

Nazari   The kind − you would not believe!

Yossi   Ladies and gentleman, I present you: the Paper Dolls!

On another part of stage, we dimly see −

The **Paper Dolls**, *all dressed now. They are in a prayer circle, holding hands.*

Paper Dolls (*together*)   Holy Mary, mother of God, pray for us sinners, now and at the hour of our death. Amen. Glory be to the Father, the Son, and the Holy Spirit, as it was in the beginning, is now and ever shall be world without end. Bless us O Lord for our audition.

Zhan   And we hope that Mr Nazari is gonna like it.

Paper Dolls (*together*)   And it will be very successful. In the name of the Father, the Son, and the Holy Spirit. Amen.

Chiqui (*to* **Yossi**)   Okay.

Yossi *clicks on boombox. Intro music.*

Nazari *sits watching.* **Yael** *and* **Ester** *also sit.* **Ester** *liberally drinking from a glass of wine.*

Yossi *films.*

Sally *enters in costume, singing, dancing.*

Sally (*to karaoke tape, Connie Francis style, like a call to prayer*)
Ha ah, ha ah, ha ah ah
Ha ah, ha ah, ha ah ah.

Hava nagila
hava nagila
Hava nagila venis'mecha
Hava nagila,
hava nagila
Hava nagila venis'mecha
Hava neranena,
hava neranena
Hava neranena venis'mecha
hava neranena
Hava neranena venis'mecha
Uru, uru achim.

The other four **Dolls** *enter as back-up singers.*

Paper Dolls (*four times*)
Urachim belev same'ach.

Paper Dolls *dance their version of the Hora, and sing as back-up girls.*

Nazari *is enjoying himself immensely. Laughing.* **Yael** *is in a bit of shock, but smiling.* **Ester** *is really into it. Clapping, singing along. A bit tipsy.*

*'Hava Nagila' morphs into 'Lady Marmalade' (in the style of PMC All-Stars). Each **Doll** has her own verse, and **Jiorgio** has the 'rap' verse. Towards the end, the song blends back into 'Hava Nagila' and ends with:*

Sally

Uru achim, uru achim
belev same'ach!

*Big finish. The **Dolls** all collapse on floor.*

Yossi, Yael, Ester *and* **Nazari** *clap.*

Yael *pours wine for everyone. Then they are quiet, ready to hear* **Nazari**'s *pronouncement.*

Nazari (*pacing*)   You are all – very good. Very funny, too. Sometimes it's not staying on the . . . right notes, but, perhaps we can do something professional. Maybe we can go to some room in my club and sit again and talk about how to make it more – amazing. So, we take this, and we're gonna fly away to the – Philippines! You will be stars in Tel Aviv. Yes? I will make you very big.

Chiqui (*smiling, to the group*)   This is what we dreamed and worked so hard for! (*Turns to* **Yossi**.) Thank you to Yossi.

*General excitement from the **Dolls**.*

Chiqui (*to* **Yossi**)   You keep your promise.

Nazari (*stands, paces a bit*)   Yes, it is nice. Very nice. But – – this song is not exactly right for TLV. I want to do something more – 'clubby'. More for the middle-of-the-evening people. They are coming to a party, not a show. And then I stop the party and we do – something. People will know that it's the Paper Dolls. But it must mix into the party.

Yossi   They have other songs they can show to you.

Nazari (*pacing, excited, thinking*)   Yes, we can do something very nice. (*Pause.*) And I think . . . all the decoration is not Philippine, it's something else . . .

Chiqui   What else?

Nazari   This Philippine thing. This is not really working for me. So, instead? Ah! I got it – we do – Japanese! Yes, the decoration is gonna be Japanese.

*The **Paper Dolls** react, surprised, confused, to this news.*

Nazari   Everyone like Japan. Japan is, how you say – 'classy'!

Chiqui   Japan?

Yael   But they are not Japanese.

Ester (*to* **Yael**)   Oy! Der oylam is a goylem. [*The world is stupid.*]

Nazari   No, this will be good. I know this. (*Pause.*) But also – something else. I don't know if we're gonna take the whole group. I think we need to take care to do this right. I prefer to use three of the best. And I will find the right song.

Yossi *gets up, goes to* **Nazari** *and pulls him aside.*

*The **Paper Dolls** move closer to each other.*

Yossi   What's with you? Why can't they all perform?

Nazari   What's with me? Because I want it to be the way I think it should be. I want the best professionals.

Yossi   You don't think all of them are good?

Nazari   Not in my opinion.

Yossi   Please, can I talk to you outside?

Yossi *motions to* **Nazari** *and they exit outside.*

*The **Dolls** watch* **Yossi** *and* **Nazari** *leave, then:*

Zhan   What is happening?

Chiqui (*flustered*)   So, shall we do this performance?

Jiorgio   If anyone has anything to say about performing or not, say it now.

Cheska   Will Mr Nazari now choose our song? Our dance?

Zhan   Shall we not do it?

Chiqui   Sally, will you perform?

Sally   Is it for me to say? Nazari will decide, no?

Chiqui (*stands*)   I am the manager. I will decide. We will decide together. (*To* **Yael**.) Mrs Schumann, what do you think?

Yael   Me? I do not know about these things, of course.

Chiqui   But, did you like our show?

Yael   It is – unbelievable!

Ester (*a little tipsy*)   And I loved it! (*Grabbing* **Yael** *by the arm and singing.*) 'Giuchie, Giuchie, tee lai lai lai'.

Yossi *enters.*

Chiqui   Yossi! Where is Mr Nazari?

Yossi   He is gone.

Chiqui   Gone?

Sally   We do not know if we will do this thing.

Yossi   What?! There is no choice. He tells me to get your answer tonight. Which three? You decide.

Sally (*surprised*)   You think we should do what Mr Nazari says, Yossi?

Yossi (*looking at his mother*)   Yes. I think it is best. This is your one chance.

Yael (*to the* **Dolls**)   You should do what will make you happy.

Chiqui   I do not know. (*Turns to* **Zhan**.) Zhan?

Zhan   I cannot say, Chiqui.

Jiorgio (*to* **Yossi**)   Of course we do it.

Chiqui   Sally?

Sally   You do not know the answer, Chiqui?

Cheska (*trying to be supportive*)   Chiqui, we trust you.

Sally   Cheska, maybe Chiqui will decide it is not you who makes the show.

Cheska   Who will you take, Chiqui?

A pause. All look to **Chiqui**.

Sally   Chiqui, every day, since we come to Tel Aviv, we speak to each other. Korek? [*Am I correct?*] Sometimes two, three times every day. All of us. Our mobiles ring. It is you, it is Cheska, it is Zhan. Tomorrow, Chiqui, who will you not call?

Dolls *look at each other.*

Lights slowly fade to black.

End of Act One.

Act Two

Klezmer clarinet.

Backlight reveals **Chasid Chorus** *surrounding* **Zhan** *at stage level.*

As **Zhan** *dresses, they sing in Hebrew the traditional Hebrew song 'Dona Dona'.*

Chasid Chorus (*sings*)
> Egel rach kashur bechevel
> Al ha'agala mutal
> Ulemala bashamayim
> Efronim mamri-im el al
> Ruach stav tzochek lo
> Tzochek umit-holel
> Tzchok ootzchok miboker or
> Ve'ad chatzi haleyl.
>
> Dona Dona Dona Dona
> Dona Dona Dona Don
> Dona Dona Dona Dona
> Dona Dona Dona Don *etc.*
>
> [*On a wagon bound for market
> There's a calf with a mournful eye
> High above him there's a swallow
> Winging swiftly through the sky
> How the winds are laughing
> They laugh with all their might
> Laugh and laugh the whole day through
> And half the summer's night.*]

During the song, **Zhan**, *in a hallway of light, changes from 'work' clothes (slacks and polo shirt) into long skirt and blouse.*

The automatic hallway lights are on a timer and flick off with a loud click. **Zhan** *turns the switch back on. This repeats several times.*

We watch as **Zhan** *performs this ritual, puts on long skirt, then removes his jeans. He takes off his polo shirt, demurely covers his chest as he puts* *on a woman's blouse, changes shoes from sneakers to high heels, and finally puts on make-up in a tiny compact mirror.*

As the song ends, he is fully dressed as a woman.

Song ends as lights click off in hallway.

Blackness. Then:

Sudden bomb explosion.

Bright lights.

Sirens. Blue, flashing lights. Screams. Panic.

We hear news reports overlapping.

Three weeks later.

Lights up on TLV dressing room.

Driving music under from next door.

Three **Paper Dolls** *–* **Jiorgio**, **Sally**, **Chiqui** *– sit facing front, as at dressing-room mirrors, applying powder etc.*

They look garish, like 'deer in headlights', and utterly unlike themselves in their Geisha outfits, and white-face make-up. They are dressed in red and gold kimonos, with chopsticks in huge black wigs.

Zhan *is powdering* **Sally**'s *face.* **Yossi** *sits nearby, involved in checking his camera.*

Zhan   So, I pass near the Carmel Market on my way here. You cannot believe it. I was there just after it happened. People are crazy from it. Screaming in the street. Pieces of glass everywhere. So many flashing lights and sirens.

Sally   We hear the sirens from here. They do not stop.

Zhan   Ambulansiya.

Yossi *(still checking footage on his camera)*   I have been by there. I suppose for a filmmaker this is lucky, but what I have seen tonight. On the sidewalk so much blood. And then a body –

and then I think maybe just an arm. And do you know who cleans up, to be sure every piece of the dead are found and buried? The Chasids! With knives and spatulas they do this. I thought these bombings were done.

He brings the camera to **Chiqui** *and indicates that he should look through at the images.*

Chiqui   Do you think they will still do the show? Maybe they close the club tonight. People will be afraid.

Jiorgio   It is crowded. Can you hear? Mr Nazari say to me, he will not close. That people should have a place to be. To keep doing their life. To forget what is outside.

Sally (*to* **Chiqui**)   When is Cheska coming? Do you know? I try her mobile but no answer.

Zhan   You know Cheska – her card always runs down. (*Trying to lighten up the mood.*) Maybe she finds a sexy Yeshiva boy.

Zhan *opens his make-up compact and begins powdering his nose.*

Yossi (*stands and looks at the* **Dolls** *for first time*)   Well. Look at you. (*To* **Zhan**.) They are amazing, no? (*He moves to* **Zhan**.) Are you – ? What I mean – you feel all right that you are not doing the show?

Zhan   I am fine, Yossi, because I am with my friends.

Yossi   And Cheska? He is fine? Where is he?

Zhan   I hope she comes.

Yossi   Why would he not come? Is there a problem between – ?

Zhan (*getting angry*)   It's private, Yossi. You don't need to know everything. (*Pause, trying to make up.*) You know, gays are like that. We have an attitude. Gay attitudes are crazy. Sometimes we are cuckoo. Craziness in our minds. Then, we will be together and we will be friends again.

Yossi (*looking at the* **Dolls**)   Well. You all look – I almost do not recognise you.

Nazari *enters.*

Nazari *(bellowing)*   Where are my girls? Where are my girls?
Are you ready now? Are you ready? It will have to do. C'mon.

The **Paper Dolls** *quickly assemble and find a quiet corner for their
prayer circle.* **Zhan** *joins them.*

Paper Dolls   Our Father, who art in heaven, hallowed be
thy name . . .

Nazari *(can't believe his eyes – barking at them)*   What are you
doing? Paper Dolls! On the stage now!

They stop their prayer and look up.

The club dance floor. Pounding disco intro is heard.

Strobe lights and smoke machine.

A go-go boy in tiny black Speedos dances above.

Nazari *(on echoed mic, loud)*   Get ready people. Here they are –
the sluttiest oriental lady boys this side of the Western Wall.
These girls were too filthy for Sodom and Gomorrah. And the
IDF couldn't keep them out of Tel Aviv. From the harem of
Hirohito himself. Give it up for – the Paper Dolls!

Chiqui, **Jiorgio** *and* **Sally** *shuffle out in their kimonos.*

Zhan *and* **Yossi** *follow to watch.*

Music: 'Turning Japanese' (the Vapors).

The **Dolls** *lip-sync and dance like silly pole dancers. They do
embarrassing 'oriental gestures'.*

Chorus.

Verse 1.

Chorus repeats.

*During the Chorus, they make feeble attempts to strip off their kimonos to
reveal gold bustiers underneath. Humiliating stereotypic racial gestures.*

It gets worse and worse as the song comes to a close. You can feel it is a flop.

Yossi *is filming.*

Lights out.

Paper Dolls *shuffle offstage for dressing room.*

Nazari (*voice on mic*)   And now the hottest mixes in the Middle East. Direct from Berlin. Heeerre's – Deejay Tommy!

Thumping disco/electronic music under.

Dressing room.

The **Dolls** *sit dejectedly at mirror,* **Sally** *already changing out of costume.*

Yossi *enters dressing room with his camera.*

Yossi (*trying to be upbeat*)   Sally, you were great. All of you. / So –

Nazari (*yelling from outside dressing room*)   Where are they? Where are they?

He opens door to dressing room and comes in and grabs them upright. **Zhan** *enters behind him.*

Nazari (*barking at the* **Dolls**)   Come back inside. Come in to the party. People pay good money to get you as entertainment. So – you – (*to* **Jiorgio**) on the bar! Get people to buy drinks for you. Put back on the kimono. (*To* **Chiqui.**) Come with me and I'll tell you what to do, okay? You can sit on the bar, flirting, walk around. When people come in you can say 'Herro' – like this. Bow . . . (*He mimes to them bowing like a Geisha.*)

Chiqui *and* **Jiorgio** *stand and begin to follow* **Nazari** *out.*

Sally *is out of her costume and sits at mirror. She begins to scrape white face off.*

Nazari   Sally? What are you doing? You too. Now.

Sally (*looks to* **Yossi** *and then to* **Nazari**)   No. Not like that. I will not.

Jiorgio (*looking to* **Yossi**)   Sally.

Chiqui   We make agreement to do this, Sally.

Jiorgio   It is just for now.

Sally (*to* **Chiqui**)   I do not agree to this. (*To* **Yossi**.) Is this what you want for us? This is your idea? You want to make movies of us – like this?

Yossi *just stands, saying nothing.*

Nazari (*to* **Sally**)   If you do not come, you will not be paid, and then it is over for all of you at TLV. (*To* **Yossi**.) Get your friend out there, or as far as your film? You can just forget it.

Nazari *exits.*

Chiqui (*imploring*)   Sally! We are together.

Sally   No, Chiqui. (*Pointing at* **Zhan**.) No, we are not. This no more matters. Go.

Chiqui *and* **Jiorgio** *follow* **Nazari** *out to the club dance floor.*

Sally   Go, Yossi. I want you to go and watch Chiqui and Jiorgio – out there. Make your movie.

Zhan (*puts hand on* **Sally**'s *shoulder*)   Sally –

Sally   Yossi, why you only film us when we dress up? You say you make a documentary film. This means you show real things, yes? But you never make pictures when we work, in B'nei Brak. With our old men. Why is this?

Yossi *says nothing.*

Sally   Give to me your camera.

Yossi   I don't –

Sally   I want to make a movie too.

Yossi *slowly hands over the camera.*

Sally   How do you work it? Is it on? Like this. The red one?

She holds up the camera and points it at **Yossi**.

Sally (*to* **Yossi**)   Smile for me. Tell to me, Mr Schumann, you like the Paper Dolls?

Yossi (*feeling awkward but going along with it*)   Yes, of course.

Sally   And so, you will give work to the Paper Dolls?

Yossi   Of course I will give them jobs. (*Looking at* **Zhan**.) All of them.

Sally   You will hire all of us? To take care of your mama? You will give us job to take care of Yael when she is old?

Yossi *just stares.* **Sally** *points camera towards* **Zhan**.

Sally   Hello, Zhan!

Zhan *waves to camera.*

Sally   How do you feel tonight?

Zhan (*not clear what is happening*)   Very nice, thank you.

Sally   Are you happy that you are no more a Paper Doll? That Yossi makes it happen so you and Cheska can no more be with us?

Zhan   Sally!

Zhan *begins to cry.* **Sally** *stops filming, hands camera back to* **Yossi**.

Sally (*standing*)   Are you done also with Jiorgio, Yossi? Done with your oriental boy?

She grabs her bag and exits out the street door.

Out in the club, we hear the blare of techno music.

We see **Nazari** *who manipulates* **Chiqui** *and* **Jiorgio** *to stand together and bow like Japanese schoolgirls.*

Gay sex videos projected. The **Dolls** *bow over and over again, first in one direction then another, mindlessly.*

Yossi *stands in dressing room, frozen, camera in hand.*

Zhan *moves into the club.*

The area outside the club. It is illuminated with blue flashing lights.

Sally *is in the street, in street clothes. She is approached by a uniformed* **Policeman**.

Policeman (*to* **Sally**)   Hey, you!

Sally   Yes? What . . .

Policeman   I need to see your papers, your identification.

Sally   Why? I didn't do anything. I am going home.

Policeman   Your papers.

Sally   I – I don't have anything with me. I was inside the TLV.

Policeman   You will need to come with me.

Sally   My visa. My papers. They are at home.

Policeman   Where is your home?

Sally *begins to run. The* **Policeman** *grabs her.*

Policeman   That was a mistake, my friend.

He handcuffs **Sally**.

Sally (*pleading*)   Where am I going? No, please . . . I . . . My friends are inside there.

Policeman   Do not resist. It will be worse for you.

Sally   My friends! They will worry. Please!

Policeman (*stops*)   You say you have friends inside? Show me. And maybe I can let you go.

Sally, *tormented, scared, but thinking of* **Jiorgio**.

Sally   Yes, they . . . (*She stops herself*.) No. No friends. I was just saying this. It is just me. I am by myself.

The **Policeman** *leads* **Sally** *away, in handcuffs.*

Stage is filled with blue lights.

Sound of a prison door slamming.

Lights up.

The next day.

Masiyahu Prison Office.

Adina *enters and speaks to uniformed* **Guard** *at front desk.*

Adina   Excuse me.

Guard *holds up his hand to stop her. She waits.*

Adina   I really need your help. I've been trying to reach this office for a long time. I phoned and all I got was a recording over and over again.

Guard   I need to see an ID.

Adina *(rummaging in her pocketbook for her passport)*   You have a man here. I got a call. It is a mistake. He takes care of my father . . . He is from the Philippines and he has been wrongfully arrested. I am Adina Grossman. *(Shows ID to* **Guard**.*)* We just heard from his friends that he was arrested.

Guard *(surveying ID)*   Where is he from?

Adina   I told you – the Philippines – but he lives with my father. His name is Salvador Camatoy. He is called – 'Sally'. Were any Filipinos arrested last night?

Guard   Many people were arrested. There was trouble. I will check for you.

He takes the ID, goes to his desk phone and makes call.

Adina *waits impatiently, uncomfortable.*

Guard *returns.*

Guard   Filipinos were arrested yesterday. (*Looking at paperwork.*) Outside a club called TLV.

Adina   Outside a club, yes. This is the man, I am sure.

Guard   It may or may not be. We do this every day. This is our job. You will need to speak to the coordinator. Please sit and wait.

Adina   Will I get an answer? And they'll tell me what's happening?

Guard   She'll check if he was deported already, or not.

Adina   Deported! No, no! This is impossible! He is legal. He has work. I / know this –

Guard (*condescending*)   Why are you this excited!? You will get more – if you calm down.

Female Administrator *enters, and* **Guard** *points her to* **Adina**.

Female Administrator   You asked about Salvador Camatoy? He is already here and he is being processed.

Adina   What does that mean – processed?

Female Administrator   It means that he's here in Masiyahu Prison. He's illegal, isn't he?

Adina   No. This is what I am trying to tell you. You make a mistake. He is employed. I have his papers here. (*Rummaging through her bag.*) From the agency.

Female Administrator   If it is a mistake, it will be fixed. Things are black – or white.

Adina   What do you mean, black or white?

Female Administrator   If he's illegal, it means he didn't meet the conditions or that his visa is invalid.

Adina   Listen to me. You have made a mistake. I am telling you, he is working. (*Rummaging in purse.*) And I believe his visa is valid.

Female Administrator   When you say, 'I believe', it becomes a 'grey area' – which doesn't exist.

Adina   This one is not grey! My father is his employer. The agency placed him with my father. Here, you can call him now – Mr Scholem. Chaim Scholem. Take the number. Call him.

Female Administrator   I cannot. I do not have authority for this . . . I'm a small cog in the wheel.

Adina (*frustrated*)   Well, who isn't a 'small cog'?

Female Administrator (*starting to leave*)   I have no idea.

Adina   Please! I must see him! I must talk to him. Can I see him – through the bars?

Female Administrator   There are no visitors here. This is a prison, not the Knesset . . .

Adina   But a man was mistakenly detained! Can I talk to him?! Ask him where our house keys are? (**Adina** *breaks down.*) You see, this man, Mr Camatoy. He takes care of my father. He cannot be sent away. (*She finally finds the papers.*) Please, here are his papers. You will see.

Female Administrator *takes the papers, and leaves.*

Suddenly **Adina***'s cell phone rings. She makes to answer it.*

Adina   Hello! Abba . . . What? I cannot hear you.

Guard (*sees phone*)   There are no mobiles in here.

Adina   It is my father! (*Into phone.*) Abba, you talk to the man here, tell him – (*Pause.*) What is it? Hello? Hello? (*She listens.*) What is that noise? Are you okay?

Guard   Give that to me!

Adina   Papa, I am coming. And – I will bring Sally with – that I promise. I cannot hear you. So much noise. (*She listens.*) Hello? Hello!? Is something wrong? Hello?

Guard   Put that away. You'd better leave now. / Make your call outside.

Adina   No! No, I will not leave. I will not leave until I see
Salvador Camatoy. What has become of this country? You –
you will speak respectfully to me! I am a citizen of the State of
Israel. I was born here. (*Losing it.*) My son served in the IDF –
and you will not speak to me this way.

Transition: sounds of traffic. Sirens. Night-time Tel Aviv.

*We hear a voice (**Zhan**) singing the opening strains, in Yiddish, of
'Rumania, Rumania', in the style of Eartha Kitt.*

*Lights up on **Chaim**'s house. **Chaim** is sitting in his easy chair,
sipping tea, surrounded by **Chiqui**, **Zhan** and **Jiorgio**. They are
wearing street clothes: hip-hugging jeans, blousy shirts. **Chiqui** has a
silk bandanna around his neck*

SONG: Rumania, Rumania (in Yiddish) –

Zhan
  Ay! Rumania, Rumania, Rumania, Rumania,
    Ruma-a-a-nia!
  Geven amol a land a zise, a sheyne.
  Ay! Rumania, Rumania, Rumania, Rumania, Rumainia,
    Ruma-a-a-ania!
  Geven amol a land a zise, a fayne.

Chaim *stares, smiles, a bit shocked.*

Jiorgio *does his best Yiddish imitation but of course it is filled with
mistakes – Eartha Kitt is their only reference.*

  Dort tsu voynen iz a fargenign;
  Vos dos harts glust kenstu krign:
  A mamaligele, a pastramele, a karnatsele –

Chaim (*chiming in*)
  Un a glezele vayn . . . !

All Three Dolls
  In Rumania iz dokh git fun keyn dayges veyst men nit
  Vayn trinkt men iberal – m'farbayst mit kashtaval.

They dance funky, shaking their booties, to:

> Hay, digadi dam . . . digga digga digga dam
> Hay, digadi dam, digga, digga dam
> Hay, digadi dam . . . digga digga digga dam
> Hay, digadi dam, digga, digga dam.

Chaim *sits, grinning ear to ear.*

Chaim (*sings*)
> Oy, gevald, ikh ver meshige!
> Ikh lib nor brinze, mamalige;
> Ikh tants un frey zikh biz der stelye
> Ven ikh es a patlazhele
>
> Hay, digadi dam . . . digga digga digga dam
> Hay, digadi dam, digga, digga dam
> Hay, digadi dam . . . digga digga digga dam
> Hay, digadi dam, digga, digga dam.

Chaim *and* **Dolls** (*together*)
> Ay, s'iz a mekhaye, beser ken nit zayn!
> Ay, a fargenign iz nor Rumeynish vayn.

Chaim *begins to dance a little, arms in the air, Chasid-style.* **Dolls** *dance around him 'club' style. Then* **Chaim** *stands and* **Dolls** *dance around him.*

Chaim *and* **Dolls** (*together*)
> Hay, digadi dam . . . digga digga digga dum
> Hay, digadi dam . . . digga digga dum.

Sally *and* **Adina** *enter and see the weird scene in front of them,* **Chaim** *singing and dancing with* **Dolls**.

Chaim *and* **Dolls** (*together*)
> Hay, digadi dam . . . digga digga digga dum
> Hay, digadi dam . . . digga digga dum
> Hay, digadi dam . . . digga digga digga dum
> Hay, digadi dam . . . digga digga dum.

All Dolls: (*flourish and end*)
> Zets!

They all suddenly see **Adina** *and* **Sally**.

Adina (*rushing to him*)   Papa! What is going on? I thought –

Chaim (*sits, winded*)   Friends! They come. We sing.

Sally   Papa!

Chaim (*sees* **Sally** *for first time, rasps*)   Sally! Sally!

Sally *rushes over to* **Chaim**.

They embrace.

Sally   It's okay, Papa, everything's okay.

Adina   Abba, what happened? I was so frightened.

Sally   Papa, are you alright?

Chaim   Of course. Should I not be? It was for you I was worried.

Chaim *looks up to* **Zhan** *and* **Jiorgio**, *who are standing nearby, whispering.*

Zhan   You are very cute, Chaim.

Jiorgio *hits* **Zhan** *on the arm.*

Zhan   Well, he is!

Chaim   Adina, I vant you should meet the 'Paper Dolls'.

Chiqui   Shalom. I am Chiqui, a friend of Sally. This is my brother, Jiorgio. And Zhan.

Awkward pause.

Zhan   We take care of old people, too.

Chiqui   When we know you will go to the prison, then we all have a meeting at my flat, and we all decide to come and visit Chaim –

Chaim   And then arrive these angels –

Jiorgio   Charlie's Angels!

Chaim   Adina, they speak a bissel Yiddish.

Adina   So I hear.

Zhan   Just a 'bissel'.

Jiorgio   When Chaim tells to us he is from Rumania, we remember we learn this song. For a wedding. In Eilat. We have the record. Eartha Kitt. I love her.

Adina   Eartha Kitt? I love her too.

Zhan *growls like Eartha Kitt.*

Knock on door. **Yossi** *enters. They all stop.*

Yossi (*to* **Adina** *who crosses to door*)   Hello.

Adina (*not sure who this is*)   Hello.

Sally   Yossi, what are you doing here? You are no longer welcome with us.

Chiqui (*placating her*)   Sally.

Yossi   I know what you must feel. And I do not mean to – I made a bad choice.

Chiqui (*steps forward*)   Yes. (*Pause.*) All of us, we make a bad choice. We also learn something.

Zhan   We need to stay in our community.

Jiorgio   This is what is for the best.

Yossi   Listen. (*He looks around.*) I have just spoken to Cheska.

Jiorgio (*upset*)   Cheska? Where is she? Again, she will not answer his mobile.

Yossi   Cheska has been arrested.

The **Dolls** *react.*

Yossi   He calls me because – he is no longer legal. His family – they sacked him.

Jiorgio   When did this – ?

Yossi   Now, he has no papers. He is in jail.

Sally   No.

Chaim   Tsuris. Tsuris. [*Trouble. Trouble.*]

Yossi   I have already called a lawyer. A good friend. He is going right now to the jail to see what he can do. I am afraid it is serious. I am on my way there to meet him now.

Sally   I must go to Cheska, too.

Yossi   They will not let you in, Sally.

Sally   If I am with you, there is a chance.

Chiqui   We all want to see her.

Yossi   That is not possible.

Jiorgio   What if this is the last time?

Zhan   How will we say goodbye?

Sally   I will go with Yossi and see what is happening. This is all right, Papa? Adina? I promise to be back quickly. (*To* **Dolls**.) We will call you as soon as we know anything.

Chiqui   We will all wait to hear from you.

Sally *and* **Yossi** *exit.* **Adina** *sits beside* **Chaim**.

Adina (*indicating all of them*)   And so – the family waits.

Chaim (*nods*)   Our little meshpucha [*family*].

Adina   I see how he cares for everyone. This – Sally.

Chaim (*correcting her, smiling, with a rasp*)   She. Yes, she takes good care.

Pause.

Chaim *takes out his notebook and pencil and writes.*

Chaim (*speaks*)   When Sally first came . . .

He finishes his note and hands it to **Adina**.

Adina (*reading* **Chaim***'s note*)   'What choice did I have? You are my only child, and you were so far away . . .'

Adina   I know, Abba. I went far from everyone.

They sit, hold hands.

Who would think, when you came here to Palestine, 1938, that this will be the *end* of our family? You and your father travel here to build a new country. But – now, look at us. Everyone is alone.

Across the room, **Jiorgio** *stares at his brother.* **Chaim** *writes a note and gives it to* **Adina**.

Adina (*reading*)   'I miss Ezra every day. Still, I cry sometimes. For my grandson. And for you. And I understand why you stay away. But, Adina – ' (*She reads and then:*) 'I – am – not – alone.'

Adina *sits with this information for a moment.*

Chaim *takes her hand.*

Female Chasid *sings seconnd half of legato version of song/prayer Shir La'ma'a Lot'.*

Lights fade on them.

A few hours later.

Sound: loud buzzing of electronic gate.

Clanging of prison doors.

Light shift.

Prison visiting room.

Sally *sits opposite* **Cheska**, *who is handcuffed. A uniformed* **Guard** *stands upstage, observing.*

Yossi *sits to the side, his backpack in his lap. His camera is inside his backpack.*

Yossi (*holding out a plastic bottle*)   Here. For you. I bring some yogurt.

Sally   Poppy seed. Your favourite.

Guard   What is that?

Sally   Only – a yogurt. He can have it?

Guard   No. It is not allowed. Give it here.

Yossi (*to* **Guard**)   It is not permitted? Why?

Guard   Absolutely not.

He puts out his hand, and **Sally** *hands it over.*

Cheska   Sally, they gave me a paper to sign that I am going home. This is propaganda.

Sally   The man in the office said I cannot speak to you about your problem, only private things, he said. Tell me how you feel. Are you frightened?

Cheska   This place is different from your home. Home – is home.

Yossi (*to* **Guard**)   Why do you have to put him in these – handcuffs?

Cheska   It is just for now. I understand because they are afraid of everything. All the bombs. They do not know that I am a very loyal person.

Sally   Where were you, when it happened? Were you out on the street?

Cheska   My family, they told me to leave. Two weeks ago.

Sally   Why did you not tell me this?

Cheska   I was ashamed. First I am no more a Paper Doll, and then I no more have my job. I was not surprised. They wanted for me to become religious. So, I stay at my flat, and I try to stay inside, but when I get depressed, I sometimes go out. I have to try to find work. I need to work, right? In order to live. And – I have to see my friends. See their big show. I

don't even care if they catch me. You are lucky to have Chaim.
Israel did not work out for me so good.

Sally   Why does God make it so hard sometimes?

Cheska   My employers . . . they are – how you say – traitors.
Something like that. You make ten good things and then you
make one mistake, all the ten good things, washed out. They
should think – we are there in the house, they should be
thankful, because if something happens to their husband or
father, we are there to help them. They do not understand that
we respect old people. Filipinos, we are devoted. We are far
from our home but we practise our culture here.

Sally   Do you cry?

Cheska   No, never. Sally, I did not even have a chance in
this country.

Sally   Soon you will see your family. Your mama, and your
sisters.

Cheska   *You* are my family.

Sally   When I was sick, you were the one who came – with
soup. I will miss you, Cheska. Like a sister.

Cheska   Sally –

Cheska *leans forward to take* **Sally***'s hands in his handcuffed hands.*

Guard   Your time is finished.

Yossi   Cheska, is there anything you want to say to the Paper
Dolls? (*He indicates to* **Sally** *that he is secretly filming.*) A message?

Cheska *'gets' it.*

Yossi *films a close-up on* **Cheska***'s face. We see this on a screen.*

Perhaps on another part of the stage, **Zhan**, **Jiorgio**, **Chiqui** *are
sitting together, at* **Chiqui***'s, watching.*

Cheska   Please, tell them, I am not a criminal. It is not my
fault. They give us no time to find a new job. Not even one
day. Not an hour. The agency should be put in jail, not us.

Tell Chiqui and Jiorgio. Remember you are two brothers.
Please love each other. And say to Zhan, just be strong. If
anything happens if you don't have visas, go home. Don't
let these things happen because it's not nice. We don't deserve
these things. Please, tell them I love them all.

Guard *takes* **Cheska**.

Cheska   And Sally, good luck to you. Be safe. Continue on
'Paper Dolls'!

Then very loud sound of a jet plane taking off.

Lights shift.

Two weeks later.

Chaim*'s house.*

Chaim *sits in a chair, dressed in an overcoat. He is writing on his pad.
A small suitcase is open on the table, and* **Sally** *is folding and placing
pyjamas in it.* **Sally** *takes a book and puts it on top of the clothes*

Sally   Papa, I put the book of poems by Yehuda Amichai in
your bag.

Chaim *bangs on table,* **Sally** *looks up and walks to him. He hands a
note to* **Sally**. *She reads it, then looks up.*

Sally   No, Papa, I did not get to say a proper goodbye to
Cheska. I am not sure what means 'a proper goodbye'.

Chaim *writes and hands her another note.*

Sally (*reading* **Chaim***'s note*)   'You are tired. Maybe now that
I have to go away, you will have more time.' (*To him.*) You will
only go to the hospital for a week, Chaim. And I will keep
busy. I will cook for you. Bring you food – my sinigang you like
so much.

Chaim *writes a note and hands it to* **Sally**.

Sally (*reading the note*)   'You need to go out. A date.' (*Looks up.*)
A date?! With a man, Papa? You would not be jealous?!

They laugh. **Chaim** *writes and hands* **Sally** *another note.*

Sally (*reading*)   'Then – with a woman. If that is what you prefer.' (*Looking at him.*) Papa, now you worry I am a lesbian!

Adina *enters carrying a bathrobe. She places it in the suitcase.*

Adina   The taxi will be here very soon. (*She kneels by him.*) Abba – does it hurt? (*Pointing to bandage on throat.*)

Chaim *shakes his head.*

Adina   You hear what the doctors say. There is a chance if you try this treatment, but you must be in the hospital. With equipment. And real nurses. Sally and I will visit you every day.

Chaim nods. Sally goes to him. He reaches over to his side, takes out a box, and holds the box and a card out to **Sally**.

Sally   What is this, Chaim?

Chaim *gestures for her to read the card.* **Sally** *opens the envelope, removes a letter and looks at it.* **Chaim** *motions for her to read it.*

Sally (*opens letter, reading*)   'My dear Sally, I understand you completely. (*A beat.*) And you know me very well, since we've been living side by side. Everyone must follow their own destiny. It so happens that suddenly, my destiny springs upon me. I am very sorry if we have to say goodbye. In this case, the best thing for me is to wish you luck wherever you be. I hope you like this.'

Sally   Papa, no. We are not saying –

Chaim *puts his hands out to shush her, and motions for* **Sally** *to open the box.*

Sally   You do not need to give me anything.

Chaim (*able to get these words out*)   You helped me. You helped me in things you cannot imagine.

Sally *looks to* **Adina** *and opens the box.*

She holds up the gift – a beautiful two-piece outfit, a skirt and matching top.

Sally   Chaim!

Chaim *gestures for her to put it on.* **Sally** *looks to* **Adina***, who nods, and then walks off with outfit.* **Adina** *sits beside* **Chaim***.*

Adina   Papa –

Chaim   I will not come home, Adina.

Adina   Of course you will. We must not give up hope. Do not make a drama. It is you who taught me this.

Chaim   You will make sure that Sally –

Sally *(calls from offstage)*   Are you ready?

Sally *comes in modelling her new outfit.* **Chaim** *indicates she should turn around. She does. He claps delightedly.*

Adina *(walks to* **Sally***, pinches her cheek)*   A sheyn meydl. [*Beautiful girl.*] (*To* **Sally***.*) Do you like it?

Sally *(looks at* **Chaim***)*   Very, very much.

Chaim *smiles.*

Adina   You know something? (*Pause.*) It needs – this.

Adina *takes the purple scarf she is wearing off her neck. She walks to* **Sally***, places it around* **Sally***'s neck.*

Adina   Now, it is perfect!

Sally   Adina! I don't know what –

Adina   Shah! As my mother would say: You should only wear it, in good health!

Sally *goes to* **Chaim** *at his chair, sits on arm of his chair. She puts her arm around him.*

Sally   Sometimes, Papa, I wonder – if I had been a young Sabra, in Israel, during the Great War, and we had met then . . .

Chaim *and* **Sally** *laugh, look at each other.*

Adina *stands, watching.*

Lights fade.

Time lapse.

Spotlight on **Chasid 1**. *As he sings the following song, several tableaux as below.*

Song: 'Another World' (in the style of Antony and the Johnsons), sung in Hebrew.

Chasid 1 *(sings, in a spot of light,* **Chasid 2** *echoing in English)*

Ani tzarich makom acher	*(I need another place)*
Ha'im emtza sham sheket	*(Will I find there peace)*
Ani Tzarich olam acher	*(I need another world)*
Achshav hazman lalechet	*(Now it's time to go)*
Od yesh li chalomot	*(I still have dreams)*
Lo ra'iti et ha'or	*(I haven't seen the light)*
Ani tzarich olam acher	*(I need another world)*
Lo rotze kvar la'atzor	*(I don't want to stop yet)*

During the song, the following tableaux take place:

Zhan *putting his* **Old Man** *to bed, rubbing the* **Old Man**'s *temples.*

Then: a bench. **Yaakov**, **Chiqui**'s *old man, with his head on* **Chiqui**'s *chest.*

Then: **Jiorgio**, *sitting on his fire escape watching people, smoking.*

Then: in a rectangle of light, **Adina** *stands with a fistful of dirt in her hand. She places it on the light.* **Sally** *enters with the scarf on her head, holding a bouquet of flowers. She places flowers beside the dirt.*

Adina *and* **Sally** *stand beside each other. Then, they clasp hands.*

Special fades on singers as song and all tableaux end.

Light shift.

Three weeks later.

Chiqui's *house. Moving day.*

Jiorgio's *big roller suitcase lies open.* **Jiorgio**, *nearby, is holding a magazine.* **Yossi** *is fiddling with his camera.*

Jiorgio   Yossi, have you seen this? (*Showing photo spread from magazine.*) It's the 'Stud of the Year Contest!' We all think you should enter it.

Yossi   What is this? Ah, yes, yes. I'll tell you who I choose. (*Points to a photo.*) Wait a minute. He's cute.

Jiorgio (*coming over*)   No, no! (*Points at another photo.*) This one.

Yossi   Are you crazy?

Jiorgio   No, because of this. (*Pointing.*)

Yossi   Because of his 'package'?

Jiorgio   Yes, his bulging lump.

Chiqui *walks in carrying clothes to pack. He sees dildo in suitcase.*

Chiqui (*picks up dildo*)   You want to take this? Maybe not a good idea. What if they stop you at Customs and go through your bag?

Jiorgio   I will tell them the truth. That I am a very lonely horny Filipina.

He grabs it and throws it into suitcase. **Zhan** *enters.*

Yossi   Jiorgio, what are the Dolls going to do without you making trouble?

Zhan   Who's going to perm my hair?

Jiorgio   I will miss you, everyone, but to tell the truth I am frightened. I do not want what happened to Cheska to happen to me. This is my nightmare – to be in prison. I have phobias on that. I will miss this country. I'm used to Israel. I know everything. I know where to go to buy anything. Nobody can fool me here.

Chiqui   Unless you're shagging him.

Jiorgio   Bitch! After so many years, you get nowhere. If you were going to another country, you can get citizenship. Not like here. Here we are really strangers.

Zhan *holds the Israeli flag like a veil, up to his nose.*

Zhan (*singing, with drama*)
  Take my hand
  I'm a stranger in Paradise –

Jiorgio *grabs the Israeli flag from* **Zhan**, *folds and packs it.*

Yossi (*laughing*)   Maybe London will be a paradise for you, Jiorgio.

Jiorgio   Well, it is where the Manpower Agency found me a job. I am very lucky.

Chiqui   Can you imagine – my brother, in London? We must all now pray for the United Kingdom.

Yossi   Where is your job, Jojo?

Jiorgio (*repeating what they told him*)   'Sage Nursing Home, Golders Green'.

Yossi   And what about Sally? What will be for Sally now?

Chiqui (*matter-of-fact*)   Sally has applied for a visa to London as well, but if she is not approved, she will go to another place.

Zhan   London. Some day, maybe we will see it, you think, Chiqui?

Yossi   Jiorgio, is it hard for you to leave your brother? Maybe this is the time to say something.

Jiorgio (*looks up at him*)   I do not need your advice, Yossi. I never did.

Zhan   Listen to Yossi, Jojo.

Bustling noise, as **Sally** *enters carrying a big cardboard box.* **Jiorgio**, **Zhan** *behind him, giggling.*

Sally   Yossi, we have something for you. Open it.

Yossi *puts down camera, opens the big box and slowly pulls out one of the big Paper Doll paper dresses.*

Yossi   What is this?!

Sally   It was Cheska's.

Zhan   We all had a meeting and we phoned to Cheska, and he decided he wanted you to have it.

Yossi (*holding the dress up, speechless*)   And, what will I do with it?

Sally   That, Yossi, is up to you.

They laugh.

Yossi   And you, Sally? What will be for you now?

Sally   If not to UK, I think maybe I go to Dubai. The pay is very good there.

Yossi   Dubai! You will you be safe in that place?

Sally   Of course. (*Pause.*) And you, Yossi? Do you think about your future? We do. (*She takes* **Yossi**'s *camera and films him.*) We all talk and decide . . . maybe, it is time for you to go live with your mother.

The other **Dolls** *laugh.*

Yossi   My mother? I am a big boy.

Sally   Yes?

Yossi (*looks at them; he has never shared this*)   You know how it is for me here in Israel. A free country, yes. But if a man – if a man does not make a family, and children, then he is . . . This country depends on this. You cannot imagine how my brothers look down on me.

Sally   It is time for you to find someone of your own. You know, the world, it is much bigger than Israel, Yossi.

She puts camera down.

Jiorgio *and* **Zhan** *lie back on sofa, cuddling, holding hands.*

Song: 'Umagang Kay Ganda'.

Jiorgio *and* **Zhan** (*sing in Tagalog*)
   Basta't tayo'y magkasama
   Laging mayroong umagang kay ganda

Pagsikat ng araw
May dalang liwanag
Sa ating pangarap, oh-oh-oh
Haharapin natin.

Chiqui (*to* **Yossi**)   It's a song of friendship.

Zhan   'As long as we are – '

Jiorgio   'Always together' –

Zhan   'Together' –

Jiorgio   'There will always be a morning – '

Sally   ' – When the sun shines' –

Chiqui   'And we have hope.'

The **Paper Dolls** *all fall on to the bed together and sing the song, in Tagalog, entwined in each other's arms and legs.*

Yossi *stands apart, begins to film, as they sing, in Tagalog, beautifully.*

Then, lights shift for music intro to 'Walk on the Wild Side'.

Yossi *exits, paper dress in hand.*

Chiqui, **Zhan**, **Sally** *and* **Jiorgio**, *each in his own special light, begin to transform into the* **Paper Dolls**.

Chasid Chorus *become their 'dressers', each* **Chasid** *with one* **Doll**, *handing her clothes and helping her to change, assisting her with make-up.*

Music over: **Chorus of Chasids** *sing (with Jewish inflection) 'Take a Walk on the Wild Side' (in the style of Lou Reed).*

Chasid 1 *sings Verse 1 and Chorus 1 to* **Chiqui**.

We watch as the four **Paper Dolls** *one by one delicately make up their own faces, assisted by a* **Chasid**. *Piece by piece, bit by bit.*

Chasid 2 *sings Verse 2 and Chorus to* **Zhan**.

Chasids (*all four together*)
  Doo do doo do doo do do doo
  Doo do doo do doo do do doo

Chasid 3 *sings Verse 3 and Chorus to* **Jiorgio**.

Chasids *hand over wigs, boa, etc.*

Sally *enters and crosses to* **Chasid 4** *who hands her her boa.*

Chasid 4 *sings Verse 4 and Chorus to* **Sally**.

Chasids (*all four together*)
  And the coloured girls say
  Doo do doo, doo do doo, doo do doo

  Doo do doo do doo do do doo
  Doo do doo do doo do do doo

  Doo do doo do doo do do doo
  Doo do doo do doo do do doo

'Doo do doos' continue and build under:

The finishing touches, as all four **Paper Dolls** *are ready.*

Zhan, **Chiqui**, **Sally** *and* **Jiorgio** *look in the mirror.*

Light shift.

Two days later.

The stage suddenly transforms into:

The Rainbow Club (neighbourhood Gay Bar).

Music. Lights. Warm laughter. Conversation.

The **Paper Dolls** *turn face front, all in outfits, and take over the end of Lou Reed.*

Paper Dolls
  Doo doo doo doo doo doo doo
  Doo doo doo doo doo doo doo doo dooooo . . .

Club applauds and goes wild.

Zhan (*wearing fabulous paper costume*)   This is the Paper Dolls'
last show. The police caught Cheska last month. He's in the
Philippines now. So, our farewell song!

Music. They dance and move and sing.

Song: 'Grace Kelly' (in the style of Mika).

Chiqui *sings lead – others back him up.*

Sally *sings Verse 1.*

Zhan *sings Verse 2.*

Chiqui *sings first two lines of Chorus.*

Jiorgio *sings next two lines of Chorus.*

All **Dolls** *sing Chorus.*

Chiqui *sings Verse 2 start.*

Zhan *continues Verse 2.*

Jiorgio *continues Verse 2.*

Sally *finishes Verse 2.*

Yossi *runs on to the stage from behind.*

He is wearing **Cheska**'s *paper gown and some bad drag make-up, a
terrible wig. He goes to centre mic.*

The **Paper Dolls** *are floored.*

Yossi, *in drag, sings 'lead' – badly, and he overdoes it.*

Yossi *sings Chorus solo (overdoing it but oddly charming).*

All **Dolls** *and* **Yossi** *together sing and repeat Chorus.*

Song ends. Club goes wild.

The **Paper Dolls** *surround* **Yossi** *screeching and laughing.*

Everyone is thrown by the over-exuberant response from audience.

Zhan   It looks like we have a new 'Paper Doll' tonight. Please welcome – Eve! (*Wild applause.*) She was taken from Adam's rib.

Jiorgio   God should have left her there!

General laughter.

Chiqui   Hello, everyone. May I say – my name is Chiqui. I am the manager of the Paper Dolls. We were five. But my friend Sally is going away, and also my brother, Jiorgio. So soon, we will be only two. (*He looks over at* **Zhan**.) And, I want to wish for Sally, a safe journey. (*Pause.*) And to my brother, all good things, in his new life, in England. God be with you, Jiorgio. (*He begins to leave.*)

Jiorgio (*onstage, he can finally say what he needs to*)   Chiqui – Sandali lang. [*Wait a minute.*]

He drapes an arm around **Chiqui**. *Both are uncomfortable.*

Jiorgio   Hello everyone. I am Jiorgio, brother po ni Chiqui [*Chiqui's brother*]. What can I say? I've never been a good brother to my brother, you know? Now I am leaving here. And I don't know kung ano ang sasabihin ko sa kaniya [*what I'm going to say to him*].

He turns to **Chiqui** *and looks right at him.*

Jiorgio   To say I'm sorry for everything I did to you. I am not prepared. I want this to come from my heart.

Goes to **Chiqui** *and hugs him.*

Jiorgio   Chiqui. Mahal na mahal kita [*I love you very much.*] You are the greatest, my inspiration, alam mo yun di ba [*you know that, right*]? (*His voice cracks.*)

The two brothers are embracing. **Zhan** *is crying,* **Jiorgio** *kisses* **Chiqui**.

Sally (*into mic, to crowd*)   Whoever wants to cry, free tissues!

She holds out a box.

Zhan (*drying her tears as only a diva can*)   Now, I'll sing for Chiqui and Jiorgio. 'Today, Today' by Sarit Hadad/

Sally   Later, na vakla [*girl*].

They all laugh and pull **Zhan** *off the stage.*

Music in background: Sarit Hadad singing 'Hayom Hayom'.

At the bar, **Yael** *and* **Ester** *with the* **Paper Dolls** *and* **Yossi** *in drag, but no wig.*

Chiqui   You liked it, Mrs Schumann?

Yael *gives* **Chiqui** *a hug.*

Ester (*to the other* **Dolls**)   I want you should all sing at my nephew Mickey's Bar Mitzvah!

Yael (*goes to* **Sally** *and hugs her*)   Sally, you will be okay?

Sally   Of course. The universe will take care.

Yael *grabs* **Yossi**. *Hugs him tight. Starts kissing him.*

Yael   Oy vey! And this one? You meshugenah. You want to give your mother a heart attack? Is that what you want? Oy! Look at you. But, I still love you, I love you, I love you. Sometimes I think, you don't know.

Yael *smothers* **Yossi** *with kisses.*

Zhan *joins the group.*

The **Paper Dolls** *laugh and laugh. They all clink their glasses.*

Yael (*to the group*)   It is Friday evening. Shabbat Shalom, everyone.

All   Shabbat Shalom!

Yael   All of you are welcome in my home, any time. Four of my sons are gone, so, maybe for tonight, I also have four daughters.

Chiqui (*pointing at* **Yossi**)   Tonight – five daughters!

Laughter.

Yael   You know I am not a religious woman. But, on Shabbat, we say a prayer for our children. That they grow up to be strong. One for boys and one for girls. Come.

Yael *gathers the* **Paper Dolls** *together and places her hands over their heads.*

Yael   Ye'simech Elohim ke-Sarah, Rivka, Ra-chel ve-Le'ah. [*May God make you like Sarah, Rebecca, Rachel and Leah.*]

She then moves to **Yossi** *and puts her hands over his head.*

Yael   Ye'simcha Elohim ke-Ephraim ve'chi Menashe. [*May God make you like Ephraim and Menashe.*]

She gathers all of them them under her hands.

May God bless you and guard you. May the presence of God be with you and give you peace.

Then she takes **Yossi** *and gives him a huge pinch on both cheeks.*

Yael   And you. Take off that shit. You make one ugly drag queen!

The scene fades as we hear loud sound of an aeroplane taking off.

Light shift.

Instrumental track of 'I Need Another Place' underscores, while over the instrumental we hear:

Paper Dolls   Holy Mary, mother of God, pray for us sinners, now and at the hour of our death. Amen.

Lights come up in another area, and reveal **Jiorgio**, **Chiqui** *and* **Zhan**, *side by side, hands joined, dressed in their outrageous costumes, heads bowed.*

The instrumental of 'I Need Another Place' continues to underscore.

On another part of the stage, high above, lights reveal **Cheska**, *who stands on a balcony, alone, staring ahead.*

Then, on another part of the stage, lights reveal a lone figure wearing a purple scarf covering her head. The figure removes her purple scarf and looks into the light. We see it is **Sally.**

Chiqui, Zhan *and* **Jiorgio** *(continuing)*   Bless us O Lord for our first show in London − and we hope that people are gonna like it and it will be very successful. In the name of the Father, the Son, and the Holy Spirit. Amen.

Sudden loud intro track to 'Girls Just Want to Have Fun'.

DJ *(loud on mic)*   Ladies and gentlemen! The Black Cap of Camden Town is proud to present − Little Bro Jo Jo. And making their North London debut, just arrived from Tel Aviv − the sassy Miss Chiqui and Miss Zhan! Put your hands together for Paper Dolls − of London!

Loud music.

Lights up on the **Paper Dolls** *in London.*

Finale song 'Girls Just Want to Have Fun' (in the style of Cyndi Lauper).

Chiqui, Jiorgio *and* **Zhan** *begin.*

The song builds − many part-harmonies.

Cheska *and* **Sally** *join.*

And entire cast eventually joins in.

Song and choreography build to finish.

Blackout.

Song List

'Venus', by Robbie van Leeuwen
Publisher: International Music Network

'Tzena, Tzena', by Issachar Miron
Publisher: EMI

'Ata Totach', lyrics by Yosi Gispan
Traditional Folk

'This is My Life', by Canfora, Amurri, Newell
Publisher: Kassner/Curci Edizioni (SIAE)

'Lady Marmalade', by Bob Crewe and Kenny Nolan
Publisher: EMI

'Dona Dona', by Sholom Secunda, Jacob Jacobs
Publisher: EMI and Mills Music Inc.

'Turning Japanese', by the Vapors
Publisher: EMI

'Rumania, Rumania', by Aaron Lebedeff
Publisher: PRS

'Another World', by Antony Hagerty
Publisher: Kobalt Music

'Umagang Kay Ganda', by Janno Gibbs, Venie Varga
Traditional Folk

'Walk on the Wild Side', by Lou Reed
Publisher: EMI

'Grace Kelly', by Mika Penniman, Jodi Marr, John Merchant, Dan Warner
Publisher: Universal and Sony/ATV

'Today, Today', by Dudu Barack and Moni Amarilio
Traditional Folk

'Girls Just Want to Have Fun', by Robert Hazard
Publisher: Sony/ATV

Methuen Drama Modern Plays

include work by

Edward Albee
Jean Anouilh
John Arden
Margaretta D'Arcy
Peter Barnes
Sebastian Barry
Brendan Behan
Dermot Bolger
Edward Bond
Bertolt Brecht
Howard Brenton
Anthony Burgess
Simon Burke
Jim Cartwright
Caryl Churchill
Complicite
Noël Coward
Lucinda Coxon
Sarah Daniels
Nick Darke
Nick Dear
Shelagh Delaney
David Edgar
David Eldridge
Dario Fo
Michael Frayn
John Godber
Paul Godfrey
David Greig
John Guare
Peter Handke
David Harrower
Jonathan Harvey
Iain Heggie
Declan Hughes
Terry Johnson
Sarah Kane
Charlotte Keatley
Barrie Keeffe

Howard Korder
Robert Lepage
Doug Lucie
Martin McDonagh
John McGrath
Terrence McNally
David Mamet
Patrick Marber
Arthur Miller
Mtwa, Ngema & Simon
Tom Murphy
Phyllis Nagy
Peter Nichols
Sean O'Brien
Joseph O'Connor
Joe Orton
Louise Page
Joe Penhall
Luigi Pirandello
Stephen Poliakoff
Franca Rame
Mark Ravenhill
Philip Ridley
Reginald Rose
Willy Russell
Jean-Paul Sartre
Sam Shepard
Wole Soyinka
Simon Stephens
Shelagh Stephenson
Peter Straughan
C. P. Taylor
Theatre Workshop
Sue Townsend
Judy Upton
Timberlake Wertenbaker
Roy Williams
Snoo Wilson
Victoria Wood

Methuen Drama Contemporary Dramatists
include

John Arden (two volumes)
Arden & D'Arcy
Peter Barnes (three volumes)
Sebastian Barry
Dermot Bolger
Edward Bond (eight volumes)
Howard Brenton
(two volumes)
Richard Cameron
Jim Cartwright
Caryl Churchill (two volumes)
Sarah Daniels (two volumes)
Nick Darke
David Edgar (three volumes)
David Eldridge
Ben Elton
Dario Fo (two volumes)
Michael Frayn (three volumes)
David Greig
John Godber (four volumes)
Paul Godfrey
John Guare
Lee Hall (two volumes)
Peter Handke
Jonathan Harvey
(two volumes)
Declan Hughes
Terry Johnson (three volumes)
Sarah Kane
Barrie Keeffe
Bernard-Marie Koltès
(two volumes)
Franz Xaver Kroetz
David Lan
Bryony Lavery
Deborah Levy
Doug Lucie

David Mamet (four volumes)
Martin McDonagh
Duncan McLean
Anthony Minghella
(two volumes)
Tom Murphy (six volumes)
Phyllis Nagy
Anthony Neilsen (two volumes)
Philip Osment
Gary Owen
Louise Page
Stewart Parker (two volumes)
Joe Penhall (two volumes)
Stephen Poliakoff
(three volumes)
David Rabe (two volumes)
Mark Ravenhill (two volumes)
Christina Reid
Philip Ridley
Willy Russell
Eric-Emmanuel Schmitt
Ntozake Shange
Sam Shepard (two volumes)
Wole Soyinka (two volumes)
Simon Stephens (two volumes)
Shelagh Stephenson
David Storey (three volumes)
Sue Townsend
Judy Upton
Michel Vinaver
(two volumes)
Arnold Wesker (two volumes)
Michael Wilcox
Roy Williams (three volumes)
Snoo Wilson (two volumes)
David Wood (two volumes)
Victoria Wood